authentic

say what you mean,
do what you want, and
be whoever the f*ck you are

(a unique path to happiness
in a complex world.)

taylor ahlstrom

Copyright © 2022 Taylor Ahlstrom.

—emdashery books—

Alexandria, Virginia.

All rights reserved. No part of this publication may be reproduced, distributed, or transmitted in any form or by any means, including photocopying, recording, or other electronic or mechanical methods, without the prior written permission of the publisher, except in the case of brief quotations embodied in critical reviews and certain other noncommercial uses permitted by copyright law. For more information or for permission requests, please go to emdashery.com.

ISBN: 979-8-9850333-3-5 (Paperback)
ISBN: 979-8-9850333-4-2 (Hardcover)
ISBN: 979-8-9850333-5-9 (eBook)

Book interior & cover design by Taylor Ahlstrom.

First printing edition 2022.

Excerpt from *Pale Blue Dot* reproduced with permission from Random House Publishing Group, *Pale Blue Dot*, Carl Sagan, (1994, reprint 2011).

For Huddy.

Because he knows the worst thing about me, and it's okay.

t.o.c.

things this book is . . . and a few things it is not 1

becoming ourselves 5

    set in stone 7

    the little voice 13

    the tree-cloud 19

    fake it till you make it 25

    our ought selves 41

    fixing our lists 53

from the outside in 63

    esteem machine 65

    being yourself on purpose 71

    this is my f*cking face 84

    #blessed 89

    the happiness inventory 92

    what would you say you do here? 101

    moving the goal posts 109

a tree-cloud interlude **121**

    the anatomy of regret 123

    on running away..132

    when things fall apart......................................136

    how did i get here? 138

from the inside out **149**

    the hedonic treadmill.....................................151

    high-hanging fruit 156

    becoming translucent....................................160

    undrama your llamas.....................................173

    how fast are your windshield wipers wiping?.................188

    communicate or die 198

    the happiness conundrum 202

    at the end of the day......................................206

epilogue..**215**

    pale blue dot..217

No, you have no responsibility except to be yourself to the fullest limit of yourself. And to find out who you are. Or perhaps I should say to remember who you are. Because deep down in the secret velvet of your heart, far beyond your name and address, each of you knows who you really are. And that being who is true cannot help but behave graciously to all other beings—because it is all other beings.

—Tom Robbins

things this book is . . .
and a few things it is not

Despite what you may be thinking, this is not a book about not giving a fuck. It is not about flipping the bird at the world so you can go live in Paris, or Idaho, or in a van down by the river. You can do those things, and Idaho is highly underrated, but that's not exactly what this book is about. It is not about walking away from everything to start a new life, though you can do that too if you want to. It's not about changing who you are—it's about embracing it. It's about how to be an authentic human on this messed up planet full of other people just trying to be human too.

But what even is authenticity? How do you find it? What do you have to do? This book is about that too. It's about redrawing the lines of who you think you're supposed to be to get to the core of who you really are. But the first steps on this journey are all the ones you've already taken. You have to start by understanding your own path to the person you've become. You have to really look at all that clutter and bullshit and pressure and judgment that have been silently shaping your life every single day . . . that have been pulling you away from that incredible, glorious, *You*. But don't worry—because no matter where you are or what you're doing, your authentic self is always there. And how you live every single day of the rest of your life is completely up to you.

Maybe you want to be a new version of You who doesn't even exist yet, or maybe you just want to be happy with the You who already does. Maybe you aren't even sure who that person is under all the decisions you've been making for other people and the fear of what they'll think.

This book is about discovering that path for yourself no matter how far you wandered down the wrong one. It's about embracing the possibility for change, even when it's the scariest fucking thing you've ever done. It's about the fear that's stopping you from quitting that job you hate or finally writing that book you're always talking about.

I am here to help you overcome those fears. I am here to help you learn that everything that has been ingrained in you about all the rules you have to follow and the person you're supposed to be may have been wrong all along. It's just really hard to see that when everyone else you know is following those same silly rules too. But the thing that nobody talks about—the juiciest secret that never gets shared—is that most of those people are equally as anxious and scared and confused as you are.

I know because I started where you are, or at least in the house next door. I have lived in every corner of insecurity—of making decisions for the sake of others, of trying to *be* somebody. I spent years in a major I didn't want to study, at a school I didn't want to go to, only to spend even more years working in a career I had no interest in. I built an entire life around pretending to be a person I wasn't to please people who never mattered in the first place. Until one day, I suddenly realized I didn't have to do any of those things; I realized how much better it was just being myself. But don't you worry. This is not a book about how to be exactly like me. You don't want to be like me. I am a clumsy collection of calamities in a dirty sweatshirt with knots in my hair that I'm too lazy to brush. But you should want to be like You, mistakes and imperfections and all.

This book is about accepting those mistakes and imperfections. It's about recognizing your insecurities and shortcomings—both real and imagined, and learning to tell the difference between the two. It's about overcoming that sinking feeling that you just aren't good enough. This is a book about discovering the reasons and thoughts and excuses that are getting in the way of doing what you want—of being who you truly are.

Every one of us is littered with flaws and regrets and admirable traits and dark, shameful secrets. And it's okay. This book is about coming to terms with all those darkened corners and cobwebbed closets and coming out clean on the other side. It's about finding the *why* behind who we are. It's about finally finding value in the things that make each one of us like nobody else.

It's about finally finding value in You.

When you do come out on the other side, you will realize that there are a million different paths to true happiness in this world, and they all have one thing in common: sharing that real, honest, flawed, weird, unique, wonderful *You* with everyone you meet. And once you allow honesty and vulnerability to drive you rather than fear and external ideals of success, you can find a brand of genuine happiness and contentment that so many people probably don't even think exists. I promise you—it does. This book is about building that happiness in your life from the inside out. It's about becoming the best version of yourself there is.

To help you on this crazy journey, this book is a little bit about my own. It follows my path of realization from giving all the fucks about what people thought about me and what I was supposed to be doing with my life to giving almost none. It is a story of shedding layers, of self-actualization, and of coming to terms with who you really are. It is a road map to letting go of the things you want to let go of and extolling some parts of you you've maybe been trying to ignore. It's about recognizing the difference between the things that matter and the things that don't.

It is about finding where you want to put those precious fucks of yours each and every day.

So if there are things that you want to change, things about yourself that you fight, or a little voice in your head that keeps telling you something's not quite right, then maybe my story can help.

becoming ourselves

set in stone

You are reading this because something needs to change.

Maybe it's something so small your mother wouldn't even notice. Maybe it's something so massive you can't possibly fathom the new life that exists within it. Maybe you don't know what *it* is exactly, but something has you scratching at your once-smooth surfaces like a freshly rising mosquito bite—and you need to find out what bit.

I had that itch once. I used to dream every day about changing my life. I used to dream about getting in a car accident on my way to work just to escape the drudgery of my existence for a few days . . . visions of any other life were my only respite. With each passing year in that life, I grew more miserable, restless, and wild-eyed at the thought of getting out. All of the things I thought I wanted became a uniform two sizes too small, cutting off the circulation to who I was underneath. The person I had cultivated was a lie. It was a skin to be torn off and tossed aside. The only thing was, I couldn't get out.

I was broke and in debt and barely keeping my head above water. I had chosen my career; I couldn't just change it now. I had a lease I couldn't afford to break; I couldn't afford to move. This was the life I had made, so how the fuck was I supposed to just up and start a new one? Change was nothing but an impossible dream, a reverie for rush-hour traffic. So I resigned myself to trying to find whatever happiness I could in the constructs of the life I had built. And in the midst of these waves of hope, despair, and resignation—looking at the life that *I* had created that felt so wrong—one question ran through my head again and again: how the fuck did I get here?

Unfortunately, far too many of us (myself included) start making the wrong choices for the wrong reasons before we're old enough to know any better. Your parents are Christian, so you go to church every Sunday. Your dad was a lawyer, so you end up in law school. And as life trudges endlessly forward, we forget to question those easily navigable paths laid out before us. You take over the family business. You go to college 'cause you're a failure if you don't. You get a job you hate because now you're in a shitload of debt with a degree in 19th-century French literature, so what else are you gonna do? You get married to whomever you're dating in your mid-twenties because *we've been together a few years now, and this is just how life works, and we should probably have a baby soon.* The path of least resistance is a difficult one to resist.

The more of these choices we've made as we grow older, the fewer we seem to have left. Choosing a university, choosing a job, and choosing a spouse are the building blocks of our adult existence. These milestones read like our resumes. Your tedious desk job, your over-priced apartment, and your mid-size sedan suddenly become the load-bearing beams of your identity in the world—whether you wanted them in the first place or not. And once these great markers of your existence are decided, they feel as though they are chiseled in stone. *I don't have experience in any other field, I can't just divorce my wife, moving is too expensive, and what's wrong with my mid-size sedan?* Nothing, the Hyundai Sonata is surprisingly roomy.

But what so often and so easily goes unnoticed is that the blur of seemingly inconsequential choices we make each day are just as much a part of defining who we are as the big ones. I may have ended up making a vast, sweeping, all-encompassing, bridge-burning, there's-no-turning-back-now kind of change, but those aren't the only kind of changes that can drastically change your life. Getting Thai food on Fridays instead of pizza, saying hi to the maintenance guy in your building, wearing that wacky sequined top your friend made fun of, or going out to eat by yourself one night—these small changes have the power to precipitate great shifts within and around us.

The outer constructs of your world don't have to change at all for everything to be completely different. For *you* to be completely different.

Somehow, we all believe that whoever we are today—no matter how old we are on this very day—is the person we're going to be for the rest of our lives. We collectively believe we've reached some final version of ourselves, and in ten years we'll like the same music and want the same things. It's called the "End of History" illusion.[1] We let these broad strokes define us and think that only quitting our jobs or leaving our shitty marriages will make a difference, but that's never true. I mean, it's a much faster way to change your life, but it's not the only way.

Whether you want to or not, whether you leave your shitty job or not, in ten years you will be different, even if you do nothing at all. What we want changes; what matters most to us changes; who we are changes. Nothing in your life is set in stone. And we can be in control of that change, or it can happen without us even realizing it.

Think about how many choices you make every day. According to some people on the internet, that number is 35,000.[2] One study at Cornell[3] found we make 226.7 decisions every day just about food. The older we are, the more of these choices we make without a second thought. We refill our water glasses; we get up to go the bathroom; we kiss our spouses

---

[1] Jordi Quoidbach, Daniel T. Gilbert, and Timothy D. Wilson, "The End of History Illusion," *Science*, Vol. 339 no. 6115, (January 2013): 96–98, https://www.science.org/doi/10.1126/science.1229294

[2] Though this sourceless (yet oft repeated) factoid seems a bit high to me, I can easily see it being in the thousands.

[3] Brian Wansink and Jeffrey Sobal, "Mindless Eating: The 200 Daily Food Decisions We Overlook," Environment and Behavior, Vol. 39 no. 1 (January 2007): 106–123, https://doi.org/10.1177/0013916506295573

goodbye. We wander down well-worn pathways never stopping to consider the lives that we inhabit. *What did I have for dinner last Thursday? What did I even do last Thursday?* We tend to forget the small stuff, but when it comes down to it, it's almost all small stuff. And that small stuff has the power to change your life. Because it *is* your life.

Those 35,000 choices aren't just things you do, they're who you are. And every day, one of those tiny choices can start leading you to the new person you're going to become. Every day you can start making your way down a different path than the one you've been walking for so long. Every single day you get to decide whether to be patient, whether to be kind, whether to hold the door open for a stranger, or whether to keep hitting the "Door Close" button on the elevator even though everyone knows that button never closes the effing door.

You get to choose the things that matter to you. You get to choose what kind of person you want to put out into the world. You can start the path to change immediately. You are in complete control of your life.

There are people who change careers in their fifties and those who get divorced in their sixties. There are people who one day decide to start sailing or finally decide to say how they feel. There are people who start taking the stairs instead of the elevator or start painting again on the weekend. And there are those who leave their entire existence behind in a momentary decision—a blind leap that whatever unknown on the other side is better than the deep ocean of their own regrets they are drowning in now. And none of those people are especially courageous or fierce or brave or fearless. They all just realized one day that taking a chance to get what they wanted far outweighed the cost of failing at it. One day they just decided to listen to the little voice inside themselves saying *it's not too late*.

Whatever it is that you want to change about yourself, whatever it is you hate about yourself, it's never too late. Maybe you think you're not pretty enough or rich enough or funny enough or insert your adjective here _____ enough. Maybe you're scared you'll never find a husband or that you already married the wrong one. Or maybe you're about to because you're scared you won't find anyone better. Maybe you hate your job, but what else would you do? Or maybe you're one of those people who gets anxiety that other drivers on the road are judging the speed at which your windshield wipers are wiping so you keep them wiping faster than you normally would—or wait, are they wiping too fast now? Maybe you always wanted to move to Paris, but what if you can't hack it? What if you have to fly home in three months and face the judgment of everyone who said you couldn't do it?

Or maybe you're just tired of feeling like nothing is the way you imagined it would be and suddenly it feels like you're running out of time.

Whatever it is you want to change, you can. You are not set in stone. So it's time you start making some choices in your life—both big and small—that will help you become the person you truly are, the person you want to be in ten years . . . the person you want to be today.

february 2008

    I am twenty-five years old. I have just shy of fifty thousand dollars of student loans from my bachelor's degree. On top of that, I have anywhere between twenty-five and thirty thousand dollars of credit card debt, depending on how good I have been. I live in Charlotte, North Carolina, and other than a few close friends and my sister, I hate this city. Like getting lost down a dead end. Like waking up in a stranger's bed. Almost everyone I know and love lives in Washington, DC, and despite my desire to join them, I know I won't be able to find a job to support myself and my debt in a more expensive city. A futile sigh escapes my chest knowing that even here, I can barely afford to pay my bills. My only comforts lie in the one-room crack den that is my apartment and the three bottles of wine I know I have waiting for me at home. Every day of my life is the same.
    Despite the massive amount of work I should be doing at a job I know I am terrible at, I leave the office at six thirty, most people still toiling away at their desks. My twenty-minute walk home is spent with headphones in my ears, letting the workday slip away slowly from my mind. It is the antithesis of driving home in rush hour traffic. Opening the door to my four-walled first-floor efficiency, I kick off my shoes and immediately remove the shackles of my business casual attire. In my underwear I head straight to the kitchen and pour a large glass of cheap red wine and let the remainder of the day wash through me with the bitter crimson. Despite the books pouring from my bookcase and stacked in careless piles around my bed, I never have the energy to read for pleasure after spending ten hours reading credit documents and toiling in Excel spreadsheets. I turn on the TV and flop onto my couch-bed. I spend the remainder of the night in this position. My boyfriend is at home. With his wife.
    Before I know it, I am drunk. I am drunk every night. My sleep is sporadic and fitful, waking up each hour on the hour until I see the number starts with a seven, and it is time to get up again. My Groundhog Day nightmare, my broken record existence, my lifeless life.

the little voice

In order to start making changes, to get unstuck from our ruts, we need to understand the motivations behind our decisions up to this point, both big and small. Why are you working in the job you're in? Why are you dating the girl you're with? Why are you wearing that sweater? Just kidding, I love that sweater. Wait, are you wearing it because I said I liked it that one time? No matter who or how authentic you are, chances are, you've made some big (and small) decisions for the wrong reasons in your life. Chances are, you continue to do it on a daily basis. We all do.

What we say, how we say it, how we dress, when we laugh, the car we drive, where we live, and our very aspirations are all affected by the people around us. They are affected by the cities we live in and the groups we belong to, by the various sub-sections of society we are each a part of. Society dictates why we wear shirts with buttons down the front to work instead of shirts without buttons: one is appropriate, the other is too casual. Both are arbitrary and culturally based. Society tells us that guy in the dirty t-shirt is probably lazy. Society tells women to wear makeup every day (but not too much) and hipster dudes to wear flannel and man buns. Society told guys in the eighties that mullets were cool, and we all know how that turned out. Wait, shit, are mullets coming back now? It's why we talk differently and act differently around different people in different settings. It is the masks we wear.

At their most harmless, these expectations keep our nice society running smoothly. We all agree to shower somewhat regularly and put on pants before we go outside, and that's great. But at their worst, these expectations can lead us to stay in unfulfilling relationships, chasing careers we never wanted, wearing sweaters we sort of hate. If you don't have a career on the list of acceptable, lucrative careers, people will think you're lazy or weird. Being poor is hard and sad. If you move to Paris and then give up and move back home, people will think you're a failure. Society told you that's bad too. If you wear pajama pants to a dinner party, people will whisper behind your back—or possibly even right to your face. "Oh my God, Taylor, is everything okay????"

We all agreed that these are the rules, so now we're stuck living with them. Except, that's not really true. We have lots of rules and mores in society, for sure, but most of them can be bent or broken without shaking the foundations of civilization, I promise. Most of these things on which we place huge amounts of pressure and importance don't really matter in the first place. It's only our perception of them—and our perception of what other people will think of them—that makes them seem so important. Most of what you think is normal and acceptable is just the median. It's not a prescription for who you have to be. It's just so hard to see that when everyone you know is swimming with the same current.

Here's how it went for me: Because of the privileged, white bread, middle-class life I was born into, I went to a mix of private and public schools and a good university. During college, my mom got me a summer internship at Citibank where she worked (because nepotism), and when I graduated, I had a resume full of banking experience and a basically worthless sociology degree. Let's be clear here, there was no personal choice in this internship. I was going to work at the bank, and that was that. So naturally, I got a job at a bank after I graduated because can you even name a job in the field of sociology other than "sociologist?" After that, I got an even better job at an even better bank, and man—I should have been living the dream! It was everything I was supposed to be doing. I was successful, living on my own, and making good money. I was doing what my parents and society said I should be doing, and I was doing what I believed I should be doing. So I should have been happy, right?

Instead, I was miserable. I was drowning in credit card debt from spending it all on expensive clothes that fueled both my outward and inward perception of myself. My colleagues all owned fancy homes or were my age and just purchasing their first. Their aspirations involved things such as getting promoted, making more money, starting a family, and vacationing in Aruba. I swear one guy I worked with got married just because he thought it might help his career prospects. I certainly didn't share these aspirations, and I never wanted to work in finance in the first place, but there I was in a job I hated in an apartment I couldn't afford in thirty thousand dollars of credit card debt because I just kept saying, *Okay, these all seem like things I should be doing. These are all good things.* But why? For whom? If they weren't making *me* happy, then who the fuck were they for?

The more I questioned my life up to that point, the more restless I got, the more unhappy I felt, the more I started to wonder how many other people were doing the things they were doing for the same reasons I was—simply because that's what you do. Because we were never told there was any other option. Because it feels dangerous to wade outside that safety zone, to take a path that society has deemed as something other than traditionally desirable. Especially when you're standing out on that ledge alone. And even once you hear that little voice telling you that nothing is right and it's time to get out, change feels impossible. But more than that—it feels scary.

It's scary because every single one of us cares too much what our friends think, and even worse—what strangers think. We care about our jobs and our clothes and who came to our last dinner party out of a desire for approval and esteem, or out of fear and anxiety over what would happen if we didn't. We're so scared of failure or change or judgment that we choose unfulfilled stability over a chance at real happiness. We stack ourselves up against our neighbors and friends as if every one of us is supposed to want the same things. We let ourselves become defined by who we think we're supposed to be rather than who we really are. And when we can't live up to these imaginary ideals, it hurts. We hold ourselves to meaningless standards and tear ourselves down when we don't meet them. We crave belonging so much, we're willing to sacrifice our selves for it.

Imagine if we all agreed one day that money wasn't important, and no one needed their jobs to survive, and no one would judge anyone else if they wanted to be a lion tamer or a trapeze artist. How many people would quit and join the circus? How many people would write that book they were going to write, or take piano lessons, or learn Hungarian and move to Budapest? How many people would just stay home and play video games all day and be perfectly content with that? How many people would make that great leap they've been wanting to take but haven't because they're too afraid of what lies on the other side?

We all have a little voice inside of us. You may love being an accountant or there may be a trapeze artist hiding in there, but every single one of us makes choices big and small for the wrong reasons. Every single one of us allows the pressures and expectations of the society we've created to take precedence over who we really are in one way or another. But your little voice is there, even if you can't hear it yet. My little voice had been buzzing in my ear for years before a fortuitous trip to Africa changed everything—before a single moment on safari in the Serengeti snapped me out of a prison of my own making; before I saw all the power and wonder and beauty in the world and came to the now painfully obvious conclusion that life is too short to spend it doing something you hate, to spend it being anyone other than who you are.

When you finally embrace your authentic self, there won't be a barely audible voice telling you *it's not too late*, drowned out by the endless droning of expectations you're faced with daily. When you finally find your authentic life, the expectations of others will be the white noise in the background of the life you know you're supposed to be living. You will no longer be saddled with the regret of decisions you've made or longing for paths you could have chosen or things you don't have. You will no longer be a victim of the circumstances in your life. You will be in charge of it.

march 2009

It is the second day of our safari into the Serengeti, and sheer awe is painted on the faces of everyone in our oversized crew. After three flat tires in a row, we are finally headed towards the Ngorongoro Crater. Because we are late, the sun is already setting behind the crater rim, its golden rays piercing through the sky, unfalteringly true in every direction—a glimpse of something beyond the temporal. The plains stretch in infinite freedom beyond us. We are standing in the pop-top Jeep in the cradle of humanity, and suddenly, I am overwhelmed.

Tears fill my eyes, and my breath is both shallow and great. At twenty-five years old I feel something I have never felt before. My skin is a billion cells; everything inside me rises; everything is possibility. So much beauty will suffocate me. The yellow of the sun brushes the crater rim's horizon, and I have no words, no voice. I am nothing in the vastness of this planet. My wide smile will bridge the hemispheres. I will absorb these lands. I will swallow the world. I will devour it all. I am a human again. I am a human for the first time in my life. The purpose of life surges through me in one instant—electricity, a tangible change, the weight of a knowledge that levitates. Everything that once mattered turns to dust. I am not scared. There is no question. There is no time to waste. I can never go back to the life I lived before. She no longer exists. I am born.

At home, the change is imperceptible. Eight a.m., another meeting, another daydream. I have nothing left to give to them. I have nothing left for the company that told me my apartment wasn't nice enough. I have nothing left for the boss who told me my bonus would be bigger if I dressed more conservatively, if I played the game the way they wanted me to. The meeting is over, and I head back to my desk to begin another day of plotting my escape. I read the news. I sit on Facebook. I plan trips to anywhere, to everywhere. I start applying to writing programs. There has to be a way out. This will not be my life for long.

the tree-cloud

From the moment we are old enough to choose for ourselves, we do. A three-year-old demands to wear a tutu every day for a month; a kindergartner pulls the shy girl's hair. We start defining ourselves and carving out our own existence as soon as we're given the chance. Once we enter adolescence, each year sees us faced with choices about who we want to become, what kind of mark we want to leave on the world. We can choose to be an astronaut or a hairdresser. We can choose to be cruel or to be kind.

As we continue to grow, through our teenage years and into early adulthood, our personalities begin to solidify before us. We cultivate ourselves as jokesters or party girls or straight-A students. We build relationships with friends based around these ideas of who we are. We join the football team or the chess club. We pretend to be someone we're not or someone we wish we were. We fake it till we make it. And with every decision we make, we inch closer and closer to some cemented concept of the people we are or the people we think we're supposed to become.

But where do those choices come from? How early on is the people we're going to become decided? And how much say do we have in the matter?

There is both nature and nurture in every part of us, but we are far more than the sum of our biology and parenting. Your natural temperament, your learned character, and the city you were raised in all played a part in defining your personality— your high school traumas and your college relationships and everything in between—all wrapped up into a single, hopelessly complicated package. Nature tells us that parts of our personalities were written in the genetic code that created us, but nurture tells us even that isn't set in stone.

The choices we make can literally change our genes, allowing them to express themselves in different ways, switching on and off over time. Identical twins share the exact same DNA and yet see significantly different genetic expressions when raised in different environments. The longer they are apart, the more divergent their genetic makeup becomes.[4] Your DNA may predict that you will be outgoing, but your experiences in life can amplify or diminish that trait.

Where you were born, who your parents are, the color of your skin—these are parts of our lives that we cannot choose. But even these unchoosable things provide opportunities for us to react, to make a choice. As we see the things our parents and friends and classmates value, who we choose to be begins to crystalize. We amplify the traits of ours that align with those values, and we diminish the ones that don't. We become a strange amalgamation of the personality in our DNA and the way our parents raised us and the traumas we overcame and the behaviors we believe will get us the esteem and belonging we crave.

Maybe your mom put you down so much that you're petrified of speaking your mind and the outgoing part of you got quiet. Maybe your parents doted over your sister but left you to fend for yourself, and you chose to become fiercely independent as a reaction to that. Every one of us has people who helped us become who we are for better or for worse: parents, friends, role models, your older brother, that one person who said the thing you needed to hear that stuck with you all these years.

All of these factors—from the massive to the miniscule—are building inside of you throughout your entire life. They

---

[4.] Jordana T. Bell and Tim D. Spector, "A twin approach to unraveling epigenetics," *Trends in Genetics*, Vol. 23, no. 3 (Mar 2011): 116–125, https://doi.org/10.1016/j.tig.2010.12.005.

create the person you think you should be, helping you grow and morph and change, synthesizing the parts that are truly a part of you with what will get you the most in the circumstances you've been dropped into. These expectations for ourselves we unknowingly create so early in life become the backbone of our entire existence, silently navigating every decision we make. They brought us each to the lives we inhabit today, so often without us even noticing how we got here.

>>>>>>>>>>>>

I want you to think about how your entire life came to be exactly as it is—how you came to be who you are. Imagine you're sitting on the very edge of a branch at the very top of a massive tree. Look back at the branch that you followed to get here. Now look all the way back. This tree is your entire life. It is an ever-growing tree of opportunities and decisions and circumstances and consequences, branching into every different direction imaginable—both the ones you took and the ones you didn't. From where you're sitting, you can see the other clusters of branches you didn't choose, the paths you didn't take. And you can see back down the branches that grew into the one you're sitting on now. Each choice you make, your tree continues to grow.

As you look back down your tree, try to trace it up from the trunk to where you are now. Think how each branch you followed may have changed you, shaped you, bent you towards something new along the way. Try to find those moments on your path that saw you define yourself—or redefine yourself. Not just the ones that changed your course, like the night you met your wife, but the early ones that helped shape who you are and how you see the world, your meaning-making experiences. If you're funny, why is that? If you're quiet or loud or cautious or cynical or sarcastic, were you born that way? Or was it a reaction, a response, a way to get something you needed from the world?

Follow those thick, load-bearing branches in your life through to the tiny twigs that grew from them—the new friends you met or when you started dressing a little differently. Trace who you are back to the fork that contained a different you. When did you become the person that led you to the relationship you're in now? Did you always want the things that you have? If you were born in a rural trailer park instead of a quiet suburban neighborhood (or vice versa), how different do you think you would be? How much do you believe you're a product of your environment versus a person just born to be you?

Some of our branches are moments that defined us, those meaning-making experiences. Others are just flashes, choices seared into our memories. Things we love to recall or things we wish we could forget. Some made a difference, some didn't, and some took us down paths we could never unfollow. Now imagine the branches you didn't take—opportunities missed or tough decisions made. Think about why you chose the branches you did. Or why you wish you hadn't.

Think about the thing you wish you hadn't said or that guy you shouldn't have slept with. Think about the ones you wish you had . . . like that job you passed up or the love you let slip away. My favorite branches to recall are the ones that seemed like terrible things when they happened, but that pushed you into a better path in a strange twist of fate or chance or destiny or as part of God's plan, whatever you believe.

For you, maybe there was one thick, gnarly branch in your tree of unrealized universes that contained more possibilities than any other. Maybe it wasn't even a choice, but a circumstance, an event, a curve ball of life that there was no avoiding either way, like getting laid off during the recession (which one, amirite??), or getting hit by that drunk driver, or when your dad got sick, and you had to move back home. And still you think, *if only that hadn't happened . . . things would be so much different.*

When you start to imagine what those other lives of yours could have looked like, you probably see this same exact person sitting here reading, except your dad never got sick or you studied business instead of art and now you're rich instead of poor. But the branch you followed changed you. The people who inhabit your life change you. The version of you who exists in your cloud of daily decisions is inextricable from the paths that you've taken to get where you are.

So often we see our lives as a linear progression of massive decisions. Instead of a tree, it's a highway or a train, barreling down the first set of tracks we set out on from college to marriage to kids. But your life is not linear. It's an infinite tree-cloud of decision and identity. Swirling around those branches, thick and thin, is the cloud of 35,000 infinitesimally small, seemingly meaningless choices that you make each day—that make *you* each day—how you dress, how you act, what you value, who you believe yourself to be. Within this nearly unfathomable tree-cloud is everything your life is or could be. For every decision you make and have made, there is another one you didn't, and all of it is part of who you are.

The tree-cloud is a pretty crazy place.

But if you're doing it right, your tree-cloud will give you both a map to who you are today and the parts of your life you want to change—the branches you wished you had followed. You can get to the core of the things you really want to do for *you*. It can help you to see the things that just may have been your authentic self that you put away all those years ago. You can start to understand all the times that the people around you and the things that were expected of you shaped the direction you ended up taking.

To do that, you have to find the moments when you silenced your authentic self to please someone else or to fit in, or when you made a decision because you knew it was something you had to do instead of what you knew you wanted. Look for the moments that made you feel good, that made you feel great. Moments that made you feel loved and validated and seen, as well as the ones that made you feel empty and shitty and broken. Look for the ones that made you swear you'd never do that again, and most of all, look for the branches you wish you had taken—because so often those regrets are rooted in unrealized versions of our true authentic selves.

Everything you are today is connected in your tree-cloud—whether it was a time you embraced the person you were born to be, or a time you eschewed that version of you. Even the seemingly inconsequential things, even the shitty things that happened to you (often especially the shitty things), all played their part. And they continue to do it every day. The people we become, the lives we end up living, are crafted through a lifetime of choices that we are never finished making. Every day your branches grow. Every day the person you are is changed or affirmed in the mist of thousands of tiny choices you make—from closing the elevator door on a stranger to picking up the phone to call your sister.

Maybe you feel like your tree hasn't grown a new branch in a long time. Maybe you're stuck in the same cloud of the same choices making the same weather patterns all around you. Maybe you feel like your fruit already dropped and now you'll wither and die (too much tree metaphor?) But that's never true.

When you start to understand that the choices you make shape who you are, you can start to see that taking a different path, following a different branch, can always change the person you're going to become. The cloud becomes the twigs that can grow into a whole new branch of your life. All you have to do is decide which way you want to grow.

fake it till you make it

Maybe you're still having trouble understanding your path through your own tree-cloud. Or maybe you're just feeling a little unsure about everything. That's good. While there are some of us who knew they wanted to be financial planners when they were eight (yes, she is a real human I know), for most of us, the journey to who we become as adults is anything but a straight line.

We change course, we adjust the sails, we figure it out as we go along. Our tree-clouds consist of a million memories, a million moments, and a million things indelible in our own minds, most likely forgotten to everyone else in the room. Some of these things are regrets, sure. Some people are struck by tragedy and other people experience shockingly easy lives. But most of it all is just choices. Just the thousands of decisions we make every single day that slowly turn us into the people we are now, that continue to turn us into the people we're going to become.

I'm going to take you on a little journey through parts of my own tree-cloud, much of which involves my painfully awkward formative years. When I think about my path to authenticity, these are the moments that stand out. I haven't experienced any real tragedy in my life; I overcame no great loss. But I still grew from something—from this mess of memories and choices and realizations that created the person sitting here writing. As you're reading, try to imagine your own path. Connect the dots from who you were when you were ten to your teenage years to college (or not college) and today. Who made an impact on you? Which moments do you think defined you? Did you use to be a different person when you were younger? Did you leave a version of yourself behind? What changed? And more importantly, why?

For as long as I can remember, I have been weird. Of course, I didn't always know I was weird at the time. I guess it can't occur to you that you aren't normal before you develop a solid definition of what other people think that is. How blissful were those early years before I became aware that I was uncool? And then once you realize everyone else thinks you're weird you can cue years of debilitating anxiety over it. Anxiety that led me to therapy in ninth grade, anxiety that led me to drop out of public school and into homeschool for a year. Anxiety that indirectly led to years of semi-serious drug addiction that stayed with me through high school and which I didn't fully kick until my mid-twenties. Don't worry, I'm good now.

But through all those veiled attempts at being "normal" and "cool" it wasn't until I was much older that I was able to look back at my childhood and say, *Hey Taylor, maybe you were just a weird kid.* It took even longer for me to realize the fact that I am also a weird adult. I'm not sure I can even say specifically what weird things I was doing as a child. But my family moved every year or two growing up, and no matter what town we moved to, those kids thought I was just as weird as the kids in the last town. It was a recurring theme. I didn't wear the right clothes; I didn't say the right things. I was bullied and ostracized. I was a goody-two-shoes class pet who was always the first to raise my hand. Is that weird? Or just uncool? And why is being smart uncool?

Once I left the comforts of early elementary school—where the only requirement to make a friend is to live down the street—I was always the new girl, and I was always the odd one out. I was skipped over the third grade, which both alienated me from my second-grade classmates and the fourth-grade class I was now a part of. Thankfully, we moved again. In fifth grade they called me "Rat Girl," a cruel reference to my noticeable overbite and front-and-center snaggletooth that refused to stay put even after braces. We moved again. In seventh grade, they called me "B.O." and filled my locker with deodorant despite the fact that, thanks to skipping a grade, I was still two years away from "becoming a woman" and certainly didn't smell. Or maybe I did? Who cares.

My response to these offenses was to withdraw completely into myself, hoping that staring at my feet as I shuffled through the hallways would make me invisible. They teased me for that too. They teased me for getting straight-As until I started lying on the bus about my report card, proudly claiming there was a C+ on there that didn't exist. They teased me about the scleroderma on my back when I wore a tank top and played tricks on me during lunch. Even the other decidedly uncool kids didn't want to be seen with me. As a now thirty-eight-year-old woman, I can confidently say that seventh grade was the worst year of my life. One day, while sitting alone in the cafeteria at lunch, one of the most popular boys invited me to the seventh-grade dance. I was too wary and scared to fall for that old trick, so I turned him down. But the thought, *What if that had been real? What if I were actually popular?* lingered in my mind long after. Like, years after.

Eighth grade saw me moved to yet another school, this time a charter school on Cape Cod. For the first time in my young life, I had real friends. It was okay that I was weird because we were all a little weird. It was okay that I was smart because we were all pretty smart. Alas, my parents' twisted cruelty tore me from the first happiness I had experienced in adolescence. In the summer before ninth grade, my parents announced we were moving yet again, this time from Massachusetts to Long Island. I was determined not to let it happen again. I was tired of being picked on. I was tired of being weird. Maybe being weird and unique and individual is cool now, but in the halls of high schools across America in the nineties, conformity reigned.

I decided I had no choice but to take advantage of the opportunity to completely reinvent myself. I came up with a brilliant plan . . . just stop being weird. Stop wearing weird clothes; stop saying weird things. Stop being your wonderful, kooky self. Stop doing anything that everyone else wasn't already doing. Find out however the most popular girls dressed and replicate it. I probably failed at this as I didn't have the money to buy Prada bags when I was fourteen, but I tried. No kooky shirts, no mismatched socks. I turned to my ever-popular and well-dressed sister for help. After the clothes, I deferred to the opinions of whomever I determined was the coolest person. Never dare to disagree or contradict. The safest way to be liked was to, of course, emulate the people whom you wanted to like you.

I probably don't have to tell you, but this was a terrible plan. One of the biggest tragedies of the uncool is how many of us were unable to see that *trying* to be cool is the fastest way to be definitely not cool at all. With that plan already beginning to fail, I chose the next best way to be cool in the nineties: cigarettes.

I smoked my first cigarette at the age of thirteen, standing at the edge of campus next to a chain-link fence with a person-sized hole in it that ne'er-do-wells would escape through to cut class. The hill leading down to this escape hatch was buttressed by a cement wall, the last remnants of its pale blue paint steadily chipping off. "The Wall," as it was known, was about fifteen feet long and was almost always packed with teenagers perched on its crumbling edge or milling about before class. It was where the cool kids hung out. Or at least, where the rebels did. Not the pretty, prim, and proper of the popular and wealthy Long Island elite. It was where you went to get high and cut class and chain-smoke cigarettes like the badass that you are. My older brother and sister and I would walk this way to school each morning, and each morning I would stand quietly, painfully aware that I was the only one not smoking. Most days, I would head into class a little early just to avoid the sheer terror of my own awkwardness. One day, I decided to stop being such a goody-two-shoes and join the cool kids for once. I've now been a smoker for twenty-five years (yikes).

I didn't know how to inhale for six months, but I faithfully posted up at The Wall each morning and lit up my ill-gotten contraband, blowing the un-inhaled smoke right back out of my mouth, unaware that it is very easy to tell when someone is fake smoking. I couldn't even pretend to be cool the right way. Thankfully, I was also blissfully unaware of how uncool I still seemed to be.

I continued on in this way, slowly becoming more skilled at both smoking and saying things other people wouldn't think were weird. I was cultivating the person I thought I had to be to avoid, at all costs, the possibility of ever becoming that sad, pathetic girl staring at her feet again. I started drinking in parks on the weekend and going to house parties and getting into more trouble than my parents knew what to do with a fourteen-year-old. I started doing ecstasy and acid and cocaine on Wednesday nights. I started skipping class and sneaking out and stealing the car and hooking up with twenty-year-old boys. Don't even get me started on what these adult men were doing hanging out with fifteen-year-old girls. I passed out in parks covered in my own vomit; I broke my mother's heart a thousand times. I'll spare you the rest of the terrible, regretful, emotionally scarring events that took place on Long Island, but you get the idea.

After getting sent to boarding school and getting kicked out a few months later for throwing up in the middle of an assembly; after my parents saw three of their teenage children drunk, on drugs, and skipping school; after getting homeschooled for the severe social anxiety I was suffering from; my parents announced we were moving yet again. This time, to Northern Virginia. I had spent two years practicing my cool girl persona, but all the drugs and sex and partying will still never make you cool. I left Long Island broken, still full of anxiety, doubt, and insecurity, without a single real friend to show for it.

>>>>>>>>>>>>>

But ready or not, life always goes on, and there was a new school full of strangers I had to try to become friends with awaiting me in Virginia. On the first day at my eighth new school in eleven years, unsurprisingly, I didn't have anyone to sit with at lunch. The all-too-familiar pangs of loneliness and panic sank quickly in my stomach. It was happening again. I was going to be branded on the first day as a loser, destined to eat alone until graduation. But instead of eating lunch by myself, a group of social outcasts, including a little person and a girl in a wheelchair, invited me to eat with them. They were kind and funny, and they didn't seem to care what anyone thought of who they ate lunch with. They told me the low-down on everything that went on at the school, and by all accounts, we should have remained friends. But after eating with them twice, someone who seemed cooler than they were asked me to lunch. I treated them as terribly as I had ever been treated without ever saying a word. I waved hello in the hallways for a week before pretending I didn't know them at all. The cruelties that we bear never seem to stop us from inflicting the same on others.

Despite knowing (and feeling) how wrong this was, this action was a necessary evil to me at the time. I had rationalized bruising the fingers of anyone on the ladder below me to obtain the elusive popularity that had escaped me my whole life. I refused to be the pariah for yet another year. The term "social suicide" was ringing around pop-culture back in those days—that is, the key to being popular is never to be seen with uncool people doing uncool things, such as anyone played by Anthony Michael Hall in a John Hughes movie. I sacrificed my conscience at the price of the feelings of another human, and it worked. I wasn't part of the in-crowd, per se, but I wasn't wearing the unmistakable brand of the uncool.

Pretending to be whoever I was pretending to be (I honestly had no idea who I really was at this point) was working. I played the part of the party girl—loud and fun and drunk, smoking cigarettes in the parking lot and riding around in cars with beers and boys on the weekend. Instead of being the weird new girl who stares at her feet, I was finally interesting. I had piqued their attention.

But even as I slowly made completely fake friends, I was still desperate to be accepted. My plan to be cool meant constantly worrying if anything I did or said could be interpreted in any negative way, somehow risking the precarious status I had obtained. My concept of making these friends was still based entirely upon the "dress just like them and agree with everything they say" methodology. As money is usually a prerequisite for the most popular girls in any school, I started shoplifting nicer clothes and Kate Spade bags to complete my transformation. I would shoplift extra designer bags and expensive makeup and give them to the cool girls—who, mind you, I wasn't even that close with—in order to garner their approval. How weird and ridiculous is that? They didn't seem to mind.

And through all this it never occurred to me that I wouldn't even *want* fake friends. The thought never crossed my mind that it was better when I was a loser with a single best friend who would spend hours at my house than it was to be constantly vying for the approval of a bunch of girls who were already vying for each other's approval.

I did, however, make one real best friend that year: Stephanie. She was a sophomore during my junior year, and she was not popular at all. I can't recall how exactly we became friends; I just know I never had to be anyone else around her but myself, whoever that was.

One night, in one of those regretful moments that could have come straight from an after-school special, Stephanie and I happened to drive by an unchaperoned house party. All the cool kids and their older friends who had graduated but still inexplicably went to high school parties were littered across the lawn along with their requisite red plastic cups.

"Stephanie, pull over, it's a party!" I exclaimed. The urgency of the opportunity outweighed my regard for her feelings.

"I don't really want to . . . those people don't like me."

Despite Stephanie's protests, I forced her. I couldn't possibly have missed the opportunity to party with a bunch of people who hadn't invited me to their party in the first place. I got out of her mom's van to socialize with the cool kids while Stephanie opted to stay in the parked car. Stephanie's unwelcome moniker from this crew, due to her huge puffy bangs (that admittedly never should have left 1991) was simply, "bangs." I knew that it hurt her feelings, but she always managed to throw up a steely exterior whenever they would use it. She acted like she didn't care, and I envied that about her. After a few minutes passed, the crowd of drunken juniors on the lawn finally recognized her in the front seat.

"Hey! Is that BANGS in there? Hey BANGS is that you? BAAAANGS!"

They stumbled and laughed, trying to goad a response, pleased beyond measure with their own hilarity.

Instead of coming to her defense, instead of insisting that my best friend didn't deserve this behavior—behavior that I had dreaded and endured for years—I said nothing. I brushed it off. I half-laughed at their jokes and downplayed our friendship to avoid the appearance that I was actually best friends with an uncool sophomore after school hours.

We are every decision that we've ever made.

And that moment is one that reminds me exactly the kind of person I never want to be again. It was a character-defining moment. It is the kind of thing that if someone did to me today, I would cut them out of my life. No one's approval is more important than the people who truly care about you, who are actually there for you when you need them. And if you ever find yourself ditching good friends you had for some better, richer, cooler, more beautiful people (and yes, this happens to adults too), I want you to think about Stephanie, or whoever your Stephanie is. Think about the fact that I have regretted the way I dismissed her for the last twenty years, and you probably will too. These are the only kind of regrets that still hurt decades later—the ones where you hurt a person you love. At the end of the day, those better, cooler, prettier people don't really care about you. And you shouldn't care about them.

>>>>>>>>>>>>

Not surprisingly, my bottomless desire for approval coupled with my crippling insecurity followed me straight to college. But, finally having escaped the social prison and hierarchy of high school, I felt something close to normal. I was relieved to no longer be an outcast or pariah. No one knew or cared who I was. I wasn't the new girl; we were all the new girl. No one was spreading rumors about me, and I didn't even have to shoplift a three-hundred-dollar bag for someone to hang out with me. I still didn't know who I was exactly, but who does when they're seventeen? I made friends at orientation and made friends with the hippies down the hall in my dorm. It seemed normal enough to be unsure and insecure in this vast new world, and either way, I had gotten really good at pretending I was neither of those things.

One fateful night my freshman year, I was standing at a bus stop on my way to a party with some other freshmen I met at orientation. I was wearing a pair of bubblegum pink BCBG peep-toe heels. As I stood waiting for the bus, a svelte, olive-skinned stranger came up to me and complimented my shoes.

"Where did you get those? I LOVE them!"

"BCBG," I replied with the same level of conceit that anyone who buys expensive shoes gets to display when asked where they're from.

"That's my favorite store." With her earnest reply, an invisible wall crumbled between us.

That night, Iva and I became best friends. Mark it in the tree-cloud because there is no turning back from this moment at this one bus stop all because of the shoes I was wearing. Ten years later I would meet my husband at a house party she threw.

Iva was a tall and stunningly attractive Croatian. She still is. She exudes the kind of gorgeous confidence that people open velvet ropes for without thinking. Her hair was long and thick and lustrous and always fell perfectly on her shoulders after being tousled. She had an easy, yet distinctive sense of style. Her clothes always made me wonder, *where did she even get that?* I wasn't envious of her; I was in awe of her. And she wanted to be friends with me.

Me, who didn't even know what my own style was. Me, who wasn't even sure what my personality was. Who was made fun of in every school I attended; who tried harder than anyone to be liked and to be accepted; who would do anything I could to garner that approval. I didn't know why Iva wanted to be friends with me or what exactly she liked about me, but I was determined not to screw it up. My plan? Just agree with everything she says for the rest of time. Foolproof.

About a year after Iva and I met, standing outside of a car at the both insecure and overly confident age of nineteen, I was busy agreeing with her for the one-thousandth time. The plan not to screw up this friendship was going swimmingly as far as I could tell. Iva and I were inseparable. As we stood with the car doors open, waiting to finish a cigarette, she was telling me how much she liked some actor that I didn't particularly care for. Maybe Jennifer Lopez? Ben Affleck? It was 2003, I can't remember. But despite my difference of opinion, I quickly concurred with her assessment as I had trained myself to do so diligently over so many years. And then, in a moment so mundane, in a comment so utterly obvious that most of you will roll your eyes and throw this book in the garbage upon reading it, she said:

You know, you don't always have to agree with me, Taylor.

She had found me out. She realized I had been a fraud all along. But for some reason, she didn't care. Beyond that, I somehow made it all the way to the age of nineteen before I realized it was okay to have my own fucking opinions. And even more so, that perhaps those opinions might be valuable or interesting? I had spent so long deferring to the opinions of others that it was second nature. Why would you dare disagree when agreeing on things is the basis of all friendships?! Of course, that's not true. And it took a whole lot longer before I actually assigned any worth to my own opinions. But the seed had been sown. Almost twenty years into my life, after pretending to be whomever everyone liked, it seemed like a good time to start figuring out who the fuck I really was. How much of me was really me? How much of me was built from things I had cultivated in order to please some idea of a popular person I hadn't seen since middle school? Was my entire personality a lie? Or was this the person I had truly become? As you can imagine, an existential crisis ensued.

I wish I could say this epiphany changed every aspect of my life instantly—that I was suddenly completely honest and suddenly myself. I wasn't. I still didn't even know who that was. But I was something different.

>>>>>>>>>>>>>

That same year, as the repercussions of this great epiphany were still unfolding in my tender psyche, there was a random guy I had developed a crush on. I can't even remember his name anymore (Evan? Ethan?), but he looked like the kind of person who would play a two-episode engagement as a supporting character on *Dawson's Creek*. Or maybe just an extra walking down the hallway. He was, in fact, any generic guy walking down a hallway in 2003. He wore his hair slightly spiked up in the front with gel (as was considered attractive back then), and he was forever wearing white button-downs and khaki shorts. He was one hundred percent vanilla and no other flavors. His personality matched his fashion sense.

My crush on him was short-lived as something happened that tainted my friendship with his group of friends. Whatever happened matters about as much as his name. Maybe I accidentally fucked one of his friends? Who knows. But I remember feeling disappointed. I remember vaguely wishing that something could still have happened between us and expressing this feeling to Iva. *I wish he didn't think that about me.* Iva responded to this sentiment with her signature, unapologetic wisdom.

Why would you care what that guy thinks about you? He's the least interesting person I've ever met.

Once again, Iva saves the day. Why *did* I care what he thought about me? Why did I even like him? We had nothing in common. He and his roommates were all petty, overly-testosteroned douchebags who bickered over who used more paper towels last month and then wrestled on the floor over it. When I really thought about it, I didn't care what that guy thought about anything, much less about me. And the more I started dissecting whether someone's opinion of me was valuable, the more I realized that most of them aren't.

What a miraculous and seemingly apparent thing to finally realize after you've been beating yourself into the ground for so many years! When you've convinced yourself beyond a second thought that your opinion can't possibly matter. When your entire self-perception has been based in how others view you and if you can safely say that they thought you were funny or cool or sexy or smart. Oh how the turns have tabled! To finally break the chains of approval on just a single, solitary human and, like dominoes, the rest of the inconsequential opinions I had surrounded myself with and berated myself for tumbled in turn.[5]

The more I thought about whose approval I was seeking and why, the less I seemed to care about it. The very thought of

---

[5.] I don't want to say that no one's opinion of you matters. If you're a shitty person doing shitty things, people will think you're shitty, and that matters. If you fuck your friends over, you deserve the title of shitty friend. And you deserve to lose those friends. The key here is figuring out the difference between the opinions that matter and the opinions that don't.

someone's opinion mattering began to seem utterly ridiculous. I had been fake for so many years, pretending to be a certain way to please people, that it escaped my attention that I had become someone. I wasn't pretending anymore. This was my personality. This *is* my personality. I am funny, and witty, and too loud, and too sarcastic . . . and dare I say it . . . smart. I was just so desperately insecure about those things that I couldn't see them for what they were. I was only just beginning to learn who I was and who I am, but for the first time I began to see myself as *someone*. As a person of value. As an individual existing outside the expectations of other people.

So those passing thoughts from Iva (which, by the way, she has no recollection of even though they changed my life) became the foundation for who I was going to grow into. All the lying and ingratiating and changing my clothes every time the wind changed direction . . . was that embarrassing and stupid? Absolutely. Do I regret any of it? Of course not. Maybe I could have done the right things and said the right things in school like my older sisters always managed to do. Maybe I could have fit in from the get-go and never had to spend ten tortured years lonely and desperate and confused and everything else that defines so much of our teenage years for so many of us. But then I wouldn't be me. Had I been a popular girl in high school, I probably would have ended up joining a sorority and wearing the exact same hideous belt ten thousand other girls were all wearing during those first few months of freshman year. And looking back, I wouldn't have been happy with any of that.

So when you're going through your own story (which, let's be honest, this isn't the first time you've replayed these things over the years), focus on those moments. Focus on those branches that made you—even the ones that seemed like the shittiest things at the time. Even the moments that had you doubting yourself or crying in the bathroom or wishing you could just drop out of school and never look anyone in the face again. Because so many of those are the moments that made *you*. Maybe right now you don't feel perfect—maybe right now your Iva still hasn't come along to snap you out of your prison of other people's expectations, and you still feel shitty and anxious and confused and uncertain. But don't worry. Because all of these pieces will fall into place if you let them.

august 2009

    Five months after the Serengeti, I travel alone for the first time in my life. I have no idea what I am doing. I have a cheap ticket to Mexico's Yucatan Peninsula, my backpack, and a few hundred dollars. I spend a week reveling in all the possibility there is in the world. In a strange twist I find a friend-of-a-friend who has quit his job and moved to Playa del Carmen, a laid-back beach town on the way to my destination. He invites me to come and stay with him, and I know there is no such thing as coincidence. He lives here now on almost nothing, on money he had saved. He and his roommate own only two forks. No one wears shirts in the streets. He smiles with the ease of a man who knows what he wants. I fuck him hoping he'll give me whatever it is. I think he does.
    Despite the ease of his place in Playa, I venture alone to the beaches of Tulum. I don't know how to travel yet, but I am learning. Find the cheapest hostel. Be willing to accept kindnesses from absolute strangers. Be spontaneous. Be open-minded. Be careful. I spend these days walking the beaches in a comforting solitude. I watch a couple raise their glasses in front of the moonlight-soaked sea with a soft clink. They laugh. I smile. I will never know them. I am alone—I am not lonely.
    The ocean has always held a strong influence over me, and the quiet turquoise of this ancient place pulls me ever deeper into it. I need it. But I know this is not my life. Not yet. The next day, waiting at the bus stop back to Playa, I meet a fellow traveler. An American boy, ripe with the dirt and grime of the sweaty country that we share, open to everything else we might. I will never know why, but when he asks me to return to the beach with him, I turn him down.
    I have just trekked the four miles to the bus stop with my pack. I can barely stand I am so dehydrated. I have just purchased my ticket back. A million reasons why not. Sitting on the air-conditioned bus on the way back to Playa I think of only him. I want to tell the bus driver to stop. To run back

to the beach through the stifling heat with my heavy pack on my weary shoulders just to have a beer with him. Just to learn his name.

As soon as I make it back to Playa del Carmen, I turn back to go find him. I learn how to ask for the American traveler with a red pack and curly hair in Spanish. Whatever we could have been has vanished. I never say no, but this time, I did. Whatever path that boy represented gasped its last breath as the unfamiliar words fell exhausted from my thirsty lips against his protesting invitations. I will never let caution, exhaustion, or apprehension overwhelm desire. I will only ever regret the things I don't do.

our ought selves

Now that you're contemplating this infinite swarm of everything you've ever done, not done, regretted, been proud of, and every time you closed the elevator door on someone—it's time to start thinking about each and every, monumental and insignificant, *why*. Why didn't you stand up for that kid being bullied in sixth grade? Why are you still wearing that sweater?

Of all those big, gnarly branches in your tree cloud, how many were choices you made for yourself and were things you truly wanted? How many did you make for someone else? If you did something you didn't really want to do, whom exactly were you doing it for? Was it something that made your parents happy? Did you get an apartment in a nicer neighborhood because you were embarrassed to live in the 'hood? Did you buy those boots because the Kardashians posted them on Instagram?

Of course, our motivations aren't always so clear cut. *Did I choose to go to college or did my parents make me?* Probably a little bit of both. *Did I choose my major because I was passionate about it or because I wanted to make a bunch of money?* Depends on your major and what you're passionate about. Some people are honestly really passionate about finance. I am not one of those people. *Did I marry my wife because I was madly in love with her or because we'd been together for six years and it seemed like it was time?* If you're asking that question, I think you already know the answer.

Most of the time when we make decisions, whether life-altering or mundane, it's because we believe it will be better for us—however we have defined "better" in our own personal vocabularies. Sometimes that "better" is based on an internal vocabulary of success; sometimes it's based on pleasing others or fulfilling an obligation we believe is expected of us. Sometimes it's about aligning who we think we are with the person we hope people see. Or sometimes we just try to make ourselves feel good, say by eating an entire pint of ice cream, which we then hate ourselves for, and the shame spiral commences when you know you're doing something you shouldn't. It's okay, I promise. It's just ice cream.

Whether it's what you have for breakfast or which career path you choose, each of those decisions is influenced by both internal and external factors. What society expects of you, what your family and friends want, what you really want, and what you think you should do all play into the path you end up choosing. Your family may not care what you have for breakfast, or your mother's voice may chime in the back of your head every time you reach for a bagel instead of a yogurt. We take these ideas of what we know others want from us, and we make them part of our identities.

The expectations of our friends may not be as powerful in the big decisions of our lives as those of our families, but they affect us, nonetheless. You wouldn't usually choose a career path to impress your friends, but you would certainly try a new hairstyle or buy some shoes you can't really afford (or shoplift designer bags or fly to Africa). The clothes we wear, the movies we watch, and the things we say are all decisions that our friends (or people we want to be friends with) can have a powerful influence over. Impressing the people around you is something that usually gets better with age—as in, older people tend to care way less about this than younger people do—but we all still do it to some degree. We want to be loved, we want to be accepted, so we can get stuck squeezing ourselves into an idea of a person we think will get the job done.

The self-discrepancy theory[6] developed by psychologist E. Tory Higgins breaks down the expectations we have for ourselves,

---

[6.] Higgins, E. T., "Self-discrepancy: A theory relating self and affect," *Psychological Review*, 94(3), (1987): 319–340, https://doi.org/10.1037/0033-295X.94.3.319.

our ought selves | 43

both the ones that come from what we want, and the ones that come from what our parents and friends and society want from us. He calls these expectations "self-guides." Our self-guides are the internal standards we have created for ourselves and upon which we judge ourselves. These guides manifest themselves into the ought self and the ideal self, which we compare against our actual selves.

The ideal self is who we believe we're supposed to be and who we want to be. It is our dreams and hopes and aspirations; it is our ideal version of ourselves. The ought self comes from external sources: it's the things you ought to do and who you think you ought to be. It's who we think our family, and friends, and society think we should be.[7] Note that this is not talking about what people actually expect of you in their own minds, but only what you perceive those expectations to be. You know the things these groups expect of you, and you recognize them as separate from your own internal ideals, even though a lot of the time they get jumbled together in your own head.

Our actual self is, of course, who we actually are. It is the things we say and the choices we make. But more so, it is who we believe ourselves to be. Sometimes, the person you think you are isn't the same person that the world sees you as (that's a real mind fuck we'll dig into later).

It should come as no surprise that a lot of your ought self comes from the people who nudge you along for the first twenty-odd years of your life: your parents. You spend your formative years being told to get good grades so you can get into a good school. You spend your college years working hard so you can get a good job when you graduate. That's what they told you.

[7.] Higgins refers to the ought self as a collection of our duties and responsibilities in the world versus the dreams and aspirations of the ideal self. He breaks the selves further down into own-actual, own-ideal, own-ought, and other-actual, other-ideal, and other-ought. For this book, I'm taking a slightly different and more simplistic approach between internal and external self-guides, referring to all external expectations as the ought self, or what he might call, "the other self."

That narrative is what created the ought self that led to so many of the bigger branches in the massive tree-cloud of decisions that is your life and identity.

For some, your parents may have an insane amount of influence over the decisions you make, and it's nearly impossible to stop giving a fuck what they think—to live in line with your authentic ideal self. The ought self takes the cake. Your parents want you to marry a doctor, or become a doctor, so you do those things. You do those things because walking away from those expectations comes with a hefty price tag. The intense fear of disappointment, of letting them down, can be crippling. In some cases, your self-guide is wrong, and this disappointment is imagined (your parents will still love you no matter what) and in others, your self-guide is spot on (your parents will disown you, so fuck them anyway). And for others still it can be real in a far more tangible sense, such as getting kicked out of your house or getting cut off financially.[8]

You may have gone so far down a path that was laid out for you by your family that you forgot it wasn't what you wanted in the first place. Or maybe you just convinced yourself it was. It isn't always easy to tell the difference. Internalizing, or confusing external influences for internal ones, is one of the most common mistakes we make. We take other people's expectations of us and jam them down our own throats until we forget they were someone else's idea. They often help with the jamming. It's sort of like *Inception* only that instead of being a really cool movie, it's your life and now you're wasting it on something you never wanted. Fun, right?

Your parents certainly meant well with all their not-so-subtle nudging over the years, but the path that they laid out for you is most likely based solely on external indicators of success. Think of it as "things your mom could brag to the neighbors about." For so many of us, this ought self that was being presented was

---

[8]. I promise, you don't need your parents' money.

very easy to internalize. It made sense. *Of course I want a nice house and a good job and all those things that everyone else wants.* Stereotypes of "Tiger Moms" allowing their children to become doctors and lawyers—and only doctors and lawyers—abound. Every parent wants their child to be successful, of course, but at what point does it go from a hope to a requirement? At what point are you a disappointment if you follow any other path than the one they laid out for you? How much is your ideal self allowed to deviate from your ought self?

My husband and I moved to Spain two years ago, and our neighbor here is a professional Flamenco dancer. She owns her own dance company and has been dancing for twenty-five years. But when she was ready to go to university, her father enrolled her in a program to be a pharmacist. Why? Because he was a pharmacist who owned a pharmacy of course. Never mind that Rosario hated chemistry and had no desire to take over the family business. But, she said, "My father had paid for it already. How could I say no? How could I let him down?" The turning point in her life came when it was time to take her first-year exams. Though she tried to study and do well, she failed them all. She really wasn't cut out for chemistry. She told me that she went to her chemistry professor elated and thanked him for not passing her. Because it wasn't until she failed that her father was able to realize that maybe . . . just maybe . . . his daughter really was meant to be a dancer and not a pharmacist.

If you're scared to make a change in your life because of the way your family will react, you better be one hundred percent sure you know how they will react. I went to college for engineering at one of the top engineering schools in the country. I never had a desire to be an engineer, but I was good at math and science, and my parents and teachers pushed me into it. I didn't have an alternative plan at the ready, so theirs seemed good enough. I did like physics and calculus after all, so why not engineering?

Halfway through the first semester of my freshman year, I knew it wasn't what I wanted to do. Despite knowing that I definitely didn't want to continue, I was petrified to tell my parents.

They were going to force me to stay in the program, I knew it. They had pushed me to accept a Navy ROTC scholarship (boy, did I dodge a bullet there), and they were going to push me to stay in engineering. And it's not like I had a back-up plan. I had literally no idea what I wanted to do with my education or with the rest of my life, I had just crossed one thing off my list of potential careers.

Despite my fears, I gathered the necessary courage to make the call. As the words hesitantly fled my mouth into the receiver, "I don't . . . think . . . I . . . wanttobeanengineer . . ." I trailed off without any further idea what to say, without any further idea of what to do. For just a moment, we hung on a precipice, a vast silence growing between us.

Finally, my mother answered. "Well Taylor, if you're absolutely sure that's not what you want to do, then we support you." But how would my dad respond?

"Taylor, we want you to follow your heart. If it's not in engineering, that's okay. Part of the reason you go to college is to figure out what it is that you want to do."

Did my dad really just use the phrase 'follow your heart?' The hard-lined preacher-academic who uttered things like "Children should be seen and not heard" as we were growing up? Was this really happening? I had been petrified of making this call, delaying it for weeks after having secretly withdrawn from my engineering classes. I played the call over and over in my head dozens of times, dreading their reaction and trying to come up with a good response. I thought for sure their reaction would be to first ream me and then force me to continue—at least until I had another plan.

Instead, their response could have been written for an after-school special. Instead, they supported my desire to do something that I couldn't even name yet. It was one of the most gratifying and reassuring conversations of my life up to that point. I had spent months internally freaking out about a thing that didn't even exist! Here is your daily reminder that thoughts are not facts. Points for my parents on that one.

I understand that my situation was a blessing, and that you may be absolutely positive that your parents will not tell you to "follow your dreams" when you say you're quitting school, and also, can I move back into the basement and borrow some money? But unless you're one hundred percent sure, then maybe give them the credit of a chance. They could surprise you.

Or, they could do exactly what you're afraid of. Some parents may have forced Rosario to keep working until she became a pharmacist or forced me to stick with engineering. Later, my parents pushed me into a finance career, so there's that. And others may push their children to be happy instead of wealthy or to follow a career that they're passionate about instead of one that looks good on paper. Maybe for you, becoming a lawyer or doctor was exactly what your parents didn't want, and that traditionally successful path is defying your ought self.

Let's say you come from a family who most certainly won't support you in your dream to become a traveling one-man-band. They will cut you off, there will be no money, no place to stay when it all falls out, and you can forget about coming home for Christmas. Damn mom, that was harsh.

If your parents are so sure that you should take over the family furniture-making business, or continue the legacy to Yale, or become a doctor, or a lawyer, or a professional football player because dad is still trying to relive his glory days through you, then ask yourself one question: how well do they know you?

When your parents say they know what's best for you, that may have been true when you were five years old and trying to eat an entire cake in one sitting, but is it true now? How well do they know who you are and what you want out of life? Do they know what's best for you, or do they know what's best for the average person to have a stable income and not be homeless? I am positive your parents know that an accountant has a much better chance of financial success than a street performer. But do they want you to be happy . . . or just rich? Are their expectations rooted in your own happiness or in theirs? Are they encouraging you into a traditionally lucrative career because they honestly think being richer leads to greater happiness? Or so they can tell their friends that their daughter is a surgeon? Or worse—married to a surgeon?

We often don't realize when we're young that adults are just people. In fact, a lot of us don't realize until we're thirty and it's like, *Oh shit, all those big, grown-up adults when I was little were just other thirty-year-olds also pretending they knew what the fuck they were doing.* Most people have a hard enough time figuring out what they need to do to make themselves happy. The chance that your parents know more about how to make you happy than you do is likely zero. If for one second you think they're making a good argument about upholding the family name, or continuing the family business, or whatever they think you should do, think about this: how can their expectations for who you should become be more persuasive than your own desires?

If you have no idea what you want to do and falling into the family legacy is an easy solution, I get it. I did the exact same thing. It was easier than having to make a choice of my own. But if there is even a single fiber of you that thinks you know what you want to do while you're still in high school or college or your twenties or your thirties or fucking ever—DO IT. Because that feeling, that pull, that almost silent idea that barely announced itself is a gift. It's your little voice, it's a Serengeti moment, and it's a rare thing to have. You can coast through your entire life never feeling drawn towards anything. You can have a string of jobs you don't really care about but never leave because what would you go do? So if you know, or if you think you know, go do it. And tell your parents that you're one of the lucky ones for getting the chance to do it. And if you fail, so what? You can go back and get your MBA later.

If your parents say they're going to cut you off, you can survive. I promise. You might be living in a shitty apartment with a shitty job making ends meet while you make your dream happen, but you will do it. And you will feel so much better about that shitty apartment cause it's YOURS and you paid for it with money YOU earned, and you aren't beholden to anyone. Free money is nice, but freedom is nicer.

Or maybe in your case your ought self wasn't driven by your helicopter parents, but just by society in general. Your parents told you to follow your heart, sure, but everyone you knew in high school went to college to get a job. It's weird *not* to go to college nowadays, so we just apply and get in and then figure it out from there. Never mind that some of us spent most of our college years just trying to figure out who we are as humans, leaving no time to figure out what we actually want to *do* for the next forty to fifty years. Wait, you're telling me I have to do the same job for fifty fucking years? And I have to guess correctly at the age of eighteen? *Welp, I'm sorry you guessed wrong because now you are qualified to do exactly one thing for the rest of time. Have a nice life!*

And therein lies the reason we do these things: to have *that nice life*. For most of us it's not because we love human resources or data entry or business management (though it's totally fine if you do). This ought self is easy to explain from a societal perspective: we accept innately and without question that it is more desirable to be rich and beautiful and successful than to be poor and ugly and homeless. Our ought selves created from our parents tend to align with this. You get a business degree instead of an anthropology degree because one of those things leads to money and one doesn't. Some parents may want you to follow in their footsteps, and others may only care that you are conventionally successful, but no parent is encouraging their child to explore the freedom of homelessness in their teen years.

We are bombarded with such concepts of normalcy and deviance in every TV show and across social media. *Here is what normal looks like. Here is what you should want.* We have an unrealistic idea of what this normal success looks like: an absurdly nice house (that no average millennial could afford) with a tastefully decorated living room, a loving spouse, and a couple of kids. If you're in your thirties, think about the people in your life. How many of them are married with kids and have nice steady jobs? If you're still single, do they keep asking you why you aren't married yet? If you're married without kids does everyone keep asking you when you guys are "gonna start popping some out" like you're a fucking Pez dispenser or something?

Here is what unsuccessful people look like: they live in tiny studio apartments or trailers and smoke cigarettes and drink cheap beer. They work in "menial" jobs like bartending or maintenance. If this is your life, you are necessarily unhappy. How could you be anything else? Isn't your ultimate goal to be surrounded by skinny, beautiful models and celebrities wearing ten-thousand-dollar outfits and rich dudes in Ferraris? Well, at the very least you must want a gigantic house in a nice, leafy suburb, no? No one could be happy living in less than 2,000 square feet!

While most of us know that we will most likely never be rich or famous or anything remotely resembling it, we feel pressure to want it. You may not even notice that pressure. It is so deeply ingrained and so obvious and so ubiquitous that there isn't even a question. *Of course everyone wants those things!* This pressure from society to conform into one of the acceptable molds laid out for you can be overwhelming, especially when your parents and friends are singing the same tune. Everyone is painting an identical picture of what your ought self should look like, so what else could it possibly be?

Anyone who differs from those molds will face the consequences: ridicule, isolation, poverty. We look at artists and holistic healers and people who choose to travel and people who choose to work at bars as deviants, or weirdos, or people who couldn't hack it in the "real world" as if the real world doesn't need janitors. Society views these choices as outside of the mainstream, some within the realm of acceptable, but on the fringe, nonetheless. Artists are tortured souls, musicians are either famous or broke, and no one would choose to live at a campsite or a trailer if they could have a mansion.

The issue with this is, of course, that it is completely untrue. Many people prefer campsites to mansions (myself included), and most musicians do it because it's what they love, not to become famous. Making any of these choices for your life is equally as valid as choosing to pursue a career in finance or business or law. The tiny house movement is just a way for bourgie white folks to live in a trailer without the stigma that comes with it. Choosing to care less about money, choosing to pursue an undervalued and underpaid career such as teaching or social work, or choosing to be homeless and hitchhike around the country are all perfectly reasonable ways to live your life. I promise. The problem is that you don't really believe that, and neither do your parents, and neither does most of society. Let's look at that sentence one more time: "*. . . are all perfectly reasonable ways to live your life.*" YOUR life.

So what if some strangers (or even your friends and family) think being a traveling one-man-band is weird? I think enjoying a job in a cubicle with two weeks of vacation is weird. I think buying a new car is weird. I think spending money on basically anything other than travel is weird. So it's fine if you think I'm weird. *Right back at ya, buddy.* Your decisions are for you, and mine are for me. I don't care that you're weird. Everyone is weird because no one is the same. We all have different dreams and different hobbies and different ideas of happiness. So long as the life you choose doesn't involve pillaging, raping, and murdering, you do you, boo.

I want you to think hard about all those voices in your head. Think about your mom's voice and your dad's voice and your colleagues' or friends' voices. Listen to what they are saying they want from you. Are they telling you it's time to grow up and get a real job? Are they telling you that you should be married by now or have a kid by now or have another kid by now? Are they asking you when you're gonna settle down or telling you to pursue a business major instead of fine arts?

Did you already do all those things but you're still not fucking happy?

Your ought self isn't always wrong. Your parents and friends can have some good advice sometimes. But for each of those paths, for each version of yourself they want you to become, ask yourself, why? Who does this benefit? Is this version of myself happier, healthier, wealthier, wiser? What does striving toward this ought self bring me? And most importantly, does this ought self align with my authentic ideal?

fixing our lists

It can be easy to see our ought selves as we sit in our cubicles dutifully filing TPS reports and going to fourteen meetings a week, remembering we have to pick up milk and eggs on the way home. But how do you figure out if that person aligns with your ideal self, the most important of all the self-guides? How do you define your ideal self? Where does it begin? Does it come from within you? Are you born with it? If you go on safari in the Serengeti, will it magically appear? Maybe! But that's not really how this works. Because everyone has an ideal self, even those who haven't discovered their authentic ideal yet. You're working toward something right now whether it's something that aligns with who you really are or not.

As you've begun casually pondering your entire life up to this point, have you started to understand more about how you've gotten to where you are? What built in you the values that you have today? What helped you decide the *things* that you value today? In our own hopelessly complicated tree-clouds, the pillars of our personalities that developed throughout our lives mesh and entangle with the world we were thrown into. Our ideals get created through so many events and memories and our parents and the people we grew up with, all directing us toward becoming the kinds of people we have decided have value, both in terms of who we are on paper (our careers and cars and apartments) and how we interact with people in the world and in our lives. If the exact same you were born in a different city, in a different town, you'd end up becoming a whole different version of you.

Whatever those valuable traits end up being, whether it's being funny or aloof or knowing a lot about fancy cheeses, we tend to act in alignment with those definitions. This is our actual selves striving to meet our ideal selves. We draw a picture of ourselves, and we aim to color inside the lines. *This is how I am in relationships. This is how I feel about cheese.* We understand who we are based on a list of traits and accomplishments that neatly sums us up.

Actual	Ideal
Pretty good mother	*Great mother*
Forgiving	*Forgiving*
Analytical	*Analytical*
Good listener	*Great listener*
Divorced	*Happily Married*
Part-time accountant	*Partner at a big-four firm*
Went to community college	*Went to an Ivy League*
Opens doors for strangers	*Opens doors for strangers*
Decent looking, I guess	*Sexiest woman alive*
5'2"	*5'7"*
Secretly hates fancy cheese	*Loves fancy cheese*

There are pieces of our actual selves that we know we cannot change, there are aspirations in our ideals we know we can achieve, some we know are close to impossible, and there are smaller things, smaller pieces of who we believe we already are that we are always working to confirm. Because whenever we're meeting one of these ideals we've created for ourselves, we feel good. We feel self-satisfaction. We feel at peace.

Every day we make decisions trying to get that actual to match the ideal, both in the big things and the small ones. And if we don't live up to whatever concept we have created of who we think we should be, we feel inadequate; we feel ashamed. We struggle with guilt, anxiety, and depression. If your ideal self makes $100,000 a year but you only make $50,000, then you're gonna feel like a failure. If your ideal self makes $200,000 and you only make $100,000, you'll feel the same distress even though you have twice as much money! Even if you're a perfectly wonderful accountant and wife and mother, a nagging little voice tells you, *I should have bought my own home already. I should own my own practice. I should like more kinds of cheese by now.*

This voice is a chorus of other people telling you what has value in your life. This is not the little voice we're looking to find.

Maybe your current ideal self is a successful surgeon because your father is a successful surgeon, and you internalized the ought self he presented to you, but you can't stand the sight of blood. When we internalize, our authentic ideal selves get silenced and suffocated by the weight of our ought selves. We are left dissatisfied cultivating the person we think we should be because there is still a gap between authentic ideal and real life (sometimes a massive one). We spend our whole lives wondering why getting the thing we thought we wanted isn't working.

So, what comes to mind when you think of your actual self? What traits or attributes do you think define you at this very point in time? What is your theory of your own personality? What things do you believe to be true about yourself? I want you to write down your list. You don't have to dig too deep—just how you think your neighbors or colleagues or friends would describe you.

Okay, now write down a list of traits for your ideal self. Does it feel pretty well-aligned with your first list, or is your ideal self living an entirely different life? What kind of things did you write on the list? Is everything on your ideal list rooted in money and success? Or do you put more emphasis on a sense of personal accomplishment and are less concerned with how that is perceived in the outside world? For every personality trait you wrote down as your ideal, do you already have it? Are you already that person? What about those big pillars of who you are on paper? Unfortunately, far too many of us have already internalized the ought selves that society and our families have presented to us, and so that list can get filled with things like "own more designer clothes" and "just be prettier already." But the things you write on your ideal-self list—if you're being honest with yourself—should be a window into your authentic self.

For those in the LGBTQ+ community, coming out is a great analogy for thinking about and discovering (or re-discovering) your authentic ideal self. For many who finally come out after years of being in the closet, it takes a lot of time to figure out who you really are. Which parts of your personality were you hiding or diminishing to maybe seem less queer? How much of who you have been the past decade (or more) is really you, and how much was a part you were playing to fit into the ought self you knew was being prescribed by friends and family? Coming out as gay or bi or transgender is doubtlessly much more difficult than coming out as a traveler or a trapeze artist, but the internal conflicts—and the silencing of your authentic ideal self—are the same.

If your ideal self happens to align with society's ideal—a steady career and a nice big house with two kids and a dog—that's perfectly fine too. There's nothing inherently wrong with wanting the things you're supposed to want; we just have to make sure it's coming from the right place. We need to make sure the ideal you're growing toward is a positive force for change in your life, based on things that matter and things that will actually make you happy when you get them. We need to be sure that our ideal selves aren't just based in external concepts of success and what other people think will make us happy. If your entire list is "job and house and car," then what kind of person are you going to be? What kind of person will you work to become?

>>>>>>>>>>>>

However old you are now, you've certainly gone through a few versions or iterations of yourself over the years. The list you would have written to describe yourself in high school or college is unlikely to look much like the list you would write today. For some, it transmutes more than for others over the years, but no one's ideal remains the same their entire life. If you're exactly the same person as you were in high school, then you probably have a lot more work to do than most. Think about that phenomenon where you grow up, move away for a job, and make all new friends. But when you see your old friends from high school or college, you revert back into whatever you used to be with them from before. They made a hilariously dysfunctional TV show about it called *College Buddies*.

So the you from ten years ago is maybe slightly different from the you today, or maybe totally different as you've been working towards shifting ideals. First working toward the ideal self that existed when you were eighteen, and then working toward the ideal self that exists in you now—whether or not any of these ideal selves is authentic.

While most of these changes in our ideal selves happen gradually as we get older and think more about what we want and who we are and what will make us happy, we can also take big leaps forward from time to time. Maybe that surgeon realized he could never meet the ideal he internalized and decided to open that woodworking shop he was always talking about. The kind of meaning-making experiences that lead to these great leaps—these gnarly branches in our tree-clouds—is often called a paradigm shift.

A paradigm shift represents a change in both your actual and ideal selves, in the way you see yourself and what you're working toward. At the age of twenty-eight, I believed that I would never get married after years of long-term relationships fizzling out. That defiance wasn't just an idea; it had been a part of my identity for years. I told my now-husband never to propose. But after just two years with him, somehow that crumbled. After I came back from traveling, I was a hardcore minimalist for years and believed I always would be (the End of History illusion strikes again). I had a panic attack in Target the first time I had to buy a toaster and a duvet cover. Now I cherish the art and knick-knacks and maps that fill our home.

My Serengeti moment was, without a doubt, the biggest of all the paradigm shifts in my life. It shifted my ideal self—the thing I was working toward—from this chic-yet-eclectically-dressed woman in finance to a person who wrote and traveled the world and eschewed convention. Iva may have helped the internal pieces of my personality crystallize back in 2003, but I still spent four years after college in a job I hated in a city I hated, buying clothes and furniture and art I didn't need, chasing someone else's ideal life. In that Serengeti moment, I finally started to see a bridge to happiness that brought my actual self and ideal self into the same frame for the first time in my life.

My paradigm shift changed (or rather, helped me realize) what actually mattered most to me. And with that shift, it changed the choices I was making. The tiny decisions you make each day to grow toward the person you know you want to become can immediately work to alleviate the pain of the gap between actual and ideal—the pain between authentic and ought. The way to silence that nagging little voice of your ought self is not to get a promotion or buy a nicer car or to become un-gay, it's to realign your self-guide to things that matter the most to *you*—the things that will actually make you happy and not the things you have internalized as your own desires. It's to listen to your authentic little voice and do whatever it's telling you to do.

I started taking writing classes after work; I started working toward getting my MFA, toward getting out of finance. I had a plan, and I already felt better because I knew I was working toward the thing I wanted most. Twenty-six-year-old me became vastly different from twenty-five-year-old me.

You may be wondering, *But how am I supposed to figure out what my authentic ideal is?* Well, we're working on that. But honestly, deep down in the secret velvet of your heart, I think you already know. Start by thinking about what feels the most important to you. Think about the things you might have left behind as you got older—both pieces of your personality and ambitions you once pursued. Think about the moments in your tree-cloud—probably a lot of which you've tried to stuff deep down into your psyche—that contained versions of who you once wanted to be. Think about all those times in your life when you felt great and at peace and all the times when you felt shitty and less-than.

Your ideal self can be literally anything. You don't have to move to Paris or join the circus. You can want to write more or be more generous. You can want to be a better mother or a better friend, and growing toward those things can be incredibly rewarding. Your actual self and your ideal self don't have to be in complete alignment; in fact, they shouldn't be. If they were, you wouldn't be growing.

If everything on your lists is aligned and you already have the job you want and the house you want and a lovely wife and everything is perfect . . . wait, what? Then why are you reading this book? You're here because something isn't aligned. Some part of your ideal self, your ought self, and your authentic inner voice aren't in step. If everything on your "actual" and "ideal" lists is aligned, but you still feel dissatisfied, then there is something you're not being honest with yourself about. Some part of you knows that something needs to change. We need to fix your lists.

Your little voice, your true, authentic self, may not be telling you to quit your job. You may not even be able to hear it yet. If you really can't hear it, or you really aren't sure, then we need to strip away the external influences that are drowning out the voice of authenticity inside you. We have to silence the voices of your ought selves that are creating an unbridgeable gap between who you are and who you think you're supposed to be.

We are going to peel the layers off one by one until you can finally hear what *you* are trying to say. Not everyone will have some great change to make; not everyone is hiding who they are, or has lost who they are, or is chasing some specific dream. But there isn't a single person who doesn't have something to learn about themselves. As the French philosopher Jacques Maritain once wrote:[9]

> *Things are opaque to us, and we are opaque to ourselves.*

Discovering who we are, finding the little voice, stripping away the bullshit, coming to terms with our faults, becoming better people because of it—these are parts of every single person's journey on the entire planet. It is our nature to turn a blind eye to our own shortcomings. It is our nature to see the world through the lenses of our choosing. We don't want to admit we chose the wrong career path because it would mean having to start over—and starting over is hard and scary. We don't want to admit we've been bad friends because we need to believe we're good people. We listen to what we want to hear, and we tell ourselves the same. It's the easiest way, after all. Things are opaque to us. And we are opaque to ourselves. In order to hear your little voice, in order to become translucent, we have to first learn how to be honest with ourselves. We have to admit that we've been making choices for the wrong reasons before we can make it right.

We have to start from the outside in to strip away all those oniony layers of our social masks, our feigned personas, our ideas of who we're supposed to be. We're going to start at the smallest stuff, the smallest decisions that work to define you in this world, both the appearance of beauty and the appearance of success. We're going to silence the ought selves telling you what your life needs to look like in order for you to be happy. Then we're going to work from the inside out to fully understand that who we are is what we put out into the world as human beings, not our clothes or cars or jobs or anything else. It's the relationships we foster. It's where we choose to find and assign

---

[9] Maritain, Jacques, *Degrees of Knowledge*, trans. Geoffrey Bles (London, 1959).

meaning. We're going to discover how to be happy by peeling away everything else that's been getting in the way.

february 2010

    I am sitting in seat 18F on Virgin America flight 97, non-stop from Washington Dulles to Los Angeles International. In four days, I will be on Air Pacific flight 1111 non-stop service to Nadi, Fiji. And on the twenty-fifth of February, I will be on Air Pacific flight 413 non-stop to Auckland. Three one-way tickets will take me from the truest home I have ever known to a place I have never been, and where I know not a single soul, for the next year. An inexplicable string of events has led me from the Serengeti to this moment. A month ago, this was all just a tempting joke, a crazy idea, a reckless dream, and now my plane is taking off. I press my head to the cool plastic of the window, refreshing against my skin in the stifling cabin; I watch DC miniaturize before my eyes. As eighteen-wheelers turn to ants, the white remnants of the third blizzard in this historic winter swallow the last detail of the landscape. Soon only the winding black veins of highway pavement cutting through the dirty mountains of snow around the city are visible. As we ascend, the gritty city dirty fades away, and as the snow suddenly appears as pure as the moment it fell, I whisper farewell to Washington.
    There is a strange feeling slithering around me, squeezing my limbs slow and strong as a snake. I am holding one foot over the edge, eyes wide open, more than ready to take the next step. It is excitement that electrifies my skin, tinged with nervous curiosity that tightens my belly, and pangs bittersweet when I think of the ones I love and left behind. It is a feeling that I have never felt before, and though people tell me I should be scared shitless, or making a plan, or predicting the future, I am not. I want to not know what is going to happen. I want to stumble from one place to the next as the universe guides me blindly through strangers and coincidence. I want to be ready for anything and open to everything and say no to nothing and find that something that feeds my wandering soul, that has kept my roots from searching the same soil for too long. And no part of me doubts that I will.

esteem machine

Has anyone ever asked you if you knew about a certain band, or book, or artist and you had never heard of them, but you didn't want to seem stupid, so you just said, "Yeah, sure." But of course, you hadn't, and then they asked you some follow up question, and then you felt even more stupid because you had no idea how to answer it and either had to follow up your first lie with an unconvincing second, or admit that you had just lied in the first place?

I've got some groundbreaking news for you: no one really cares whether or not you know who that band is. Also, people will think far worse of you for lying than for being slightly less cool than they hoped or thought you would be. Worrying whether or not people will approve of your knowledge of art or music or movies or fashion is like telling people you know how to juggle knives when you don't. No one cares if you can't, and lying about it will make your hands bleed.

And yet we do it anyway. We do it because we want to be accepted. We do it because the fear of rejection or ridicule is stronger than the fear of being caught in a lie. This desire to be liked and accepted isn't unique to you or me or America—it is one that we innately possess as humans.

In 1943, Abraham Maslow created his famed hierarchy of needs[10] describing basic human desires and the order we seek

---

[10.] Maslow, A. H., "A theory of human motivation." *Psychological Review*, (1943), 370–396, https://doi.org/10.1037/h0054346.

them out. First, we take care of our physiological needs like food and shelter, next we take care of safety, such as getting a job to provide for ourselves, and after that we work on belonging to a group, fostering a sense of connection with others. Makes sense. If you're starving, you're not gonna be worried about getting that promotion.

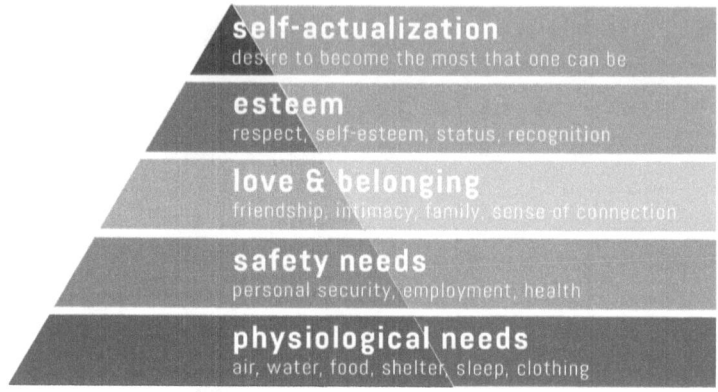

Maslow's hierarchy of needs

But we don't seek out esteem until after we've secured a sense of belonging. That is to say, feeling a sense of self-worth isn't as important to us as being part of a group. We're willing to actively sacrifice our own esteem—our own emotional well-being—to feel like we're part of something. Clearly, high school Taylor is a prime example of that. While Maslow does clarify that you can seek both belonging and esteem at the same time, you can't just jump a level. We *need* that sense of connection. We require it. Avoiding the feeling of being ostracized isn't just something we do because we like being popular; it's an evolutionary imperative. For our hunter-gatherer ancestors, being a part of a tight-knit group was more important for survival than anything else.

As an adult in our modern society, this sense of belonging probably doesn't feel like life or death. Most days you probably aren't even aware of it. You've been part of the groups you're in for so long, whether your friends or colleagues or your book club. But for every group you're in, there are still rules you play by to remain part of that in-group. It's no wonder we do all the things we're supposed to do, even at the expense of our authentic selves, in exchange for that community we so desperately crave. Just look at the flat earther movement: these guys are so tribalistic they're willing to believe the earth is fucking flat just to belong to a club.

Once you feel safe and sound in the group—once you've aligned your values with what the group values and made sure that you're checking all the boxes for membership (whether those boxes are knowing a lot about fancy cheeses or disbelieving easily provable scientific facts)—you can finally move up to the next level and start searching for the esteem you need to feel validated.

We can get this esteem from either external or internal sources: internal esteem from our own accomplishments, and external esteem from our peers.[11] Some of us are driven mostly by internal esteem such as successfully knitting your first scarf or finally running a 10k. Others crave external esteem—praise from other people—above all else. There's nothing inherently wrong with seeking external esteem (it sure feels nice), but generally speaking, the internal kind is best.

Long after the torturous insecurities of adolescence have faded—long after we've stopped lying about which bands we've heard of—we still need that esteem to drive our sense of self-worth. The failure to attain it, whether internal or external, leads to insecurity and feelings of inadequacy. Even if you told no one about your goal to run a 10k, you'd still feel shitty if you gave up. This aligns very closely with the self-discrepancy theory in that we strive to be our ideal selves and our ought selves at the

---

[11] Maslow makes a distinction between inner sources of esteem, such as a feeling of self-satisfaction and external sources like praise from a colleague: the former is "higher level," and the latter is "lower level."

same time because it makes us feel good; it gives us a sense of accomplishment and satisfaction.

We spend our entire lives chasing the feeling that comes from meeting these goals we've created—little esteem machines running around, hoping someone tells us what a good job we've done. You try to impress your date; you want to make your friends laugh. The clothes we wear, the jokes we tell, none of these things exists in a vacuum from the world around us. They are all to cultivate the esteem and validation that we naturally crave. We want to hear it from our bosses and our friends. We welcome any comments or reactions or feedback that confirm we're living up to this valuable person we've created.

Think about the list you just wrote describing yourself. If you wrote "funny" on there, can you think of a time someone told you how funny they thought you were, and that warm, fuzzy feeling rose up in your chest . . . *Gosh darnit, I AM funny!* That was a little shot of esteem you got right there.

As we age, and the groups we belong to become less fragile (or we care less about membership), we become less willing to compromise the values we've decided we're sure of. But we're still trying to live up to an image of ourselves to gain that same esteem. You may be much more confident about who you are now, your ideal self may shift less as the years pass, but you still want to hear that you are the person you've been putting out into the world, the person you've been cultivating all these years. Because part of your happiness, part of your esteem, comes from meeting the perception of who you think you're supposed to be. We spend our early lives constructing self-guides to define this ideal person within the constructs of the groups we belong to, and then we spend the rest of our lives trying to live up to those invented ideals.

But what if that ideal was the wrong one? What if you spent your life working toward the wrong thing? What if we're searching for esteem in all the wrong places?

You spend money on nice clothes because you feel like you won't get the esteem you need without them. You move into a two-bedroom apartment because it's embarrassing to be living in a crappy studio after you turn thirty. Your neighbor has designer clothes and a luxury car, and you think, *Shouldn't I have those things? I wish I could afford to get a better car.* You still scroll through Instagram every day, faced with the Kardashians and Taylor Swift (and whoever else you should immediately stop following) wondering why you don't look that way or have those things. And you want them. You go to a friend's place who has a bigger house, and you want it.

These are values that the larger group we belong to (modern American society) has defined, but they aren't inherent in who we are. They're just what we've been told has value. All of these superficial things stubbornly insert themselves as pieces of our external and internal self-guides our entire lives. These guides are constantly telling us *If you meet this ideal, you will be happy. If you look this way, you will have more friends.* But they also operate on our innate fear of being ostracized—*if you don't do these things, you won't belong.* When you go pick up the kids in sweatpants with your hair in a messy bun, your bitchy neighbor makes some snide remark reminding you to fall in line. But, as it turns out, it's all a bunch of bullshit.

For all the things you think you should be or wish you had, ask yourself, to what end? If spending a thousand dollars on a designer bag impresses people, would they like you without it? Do *you* like you without it? How much of who you are—of how you see yourself in the world—is derived from what you're wearing or your car or your ZIP code? How much of what you wear and how you act is in order to garner the esteem of others or to fulfill a concept of who you think you're supposed to be?

Is there anything you want to do, but don't because it doesn't seem to fit in with who you've decided you're going to be? With the rules and values of the groups you belong to and who *they* expect you to be?

A very successful lawyer friend of mine lives in the impossibly wealthy and conservative neighborhood of Georgetown in Washington, DC. The fiercely avant-garde and often risqué style she used to own so well in our twenties has turned into shopping solely at a painfully conservative upscale store for fifty-year-old women. Why? "Because," she says, "otherwise the other moms in the playgroup will think I'm trying to sleep with their husbands."

"Does the fact that you're not fucking their husbands matter at all in this?" I ribbed. It did not, in fact, matter.

How many unwritten rules like this are you following to keep your membership in a group that's ready to ostracize at the first sign of insubordination? And how sure are you that bending these rules will get you ostracized in the first place? And lastly, how much do you really want to be a part of a group that would banish a person based on how they're dressed?

Your unique, authentic self exists outside of these rules and expectations. You can still find the belonging and esteem you crave without sacrificing who you are. And what's more, the sources of genuine belonging and esteem you find when you stop giving a shit and stop trying to reach an imaginary ideal, are actually far more potent than the ones we've been told we should want.

As you start to unravel the groups you maybe weren't aware you belonged to, ask yourself: What will fulfilling this perception of myself ultimately achieve? And more importantly, what will defying the expectations that other people have associated with this perception cost me?

If you wore pajama pants to the dinner party, what would happen?

being yourself on purpose

In the first month of my freshman year at college, before I met Iva, I became friends with a few older hippies who lived off campus. They were juniors. They were chill, confident, laid back, and they were all obsessed with Widespread Panic. Never mind that my years in Long Island and Northern Virginia in the late nineties were spent listening to nothing but Biggie Smalls and Britney Spears. I was ready to pretend that I, too, could differentiate between different live recordings of the Grateful Dead from the sixties.

One late September night, the hippies threw a party, and I was invited. Where I grew up on Long Island, standard party attire included tight pants, a very sexy top, and some very high heels. So, I got dressed and took the bus over to the party, excited to show off my outfit and to flirt with Dan, a shy, long-haired hippie on whom I was starting to develop a serious crush. In my fluorescent blue, skin-tight pants, black floral halter top, and pain-inducing heels, I entered the party with all the confidence of the act I had perfected—only to realize that this was not a Long Island party. This was a party full of hippies in a mountain college town in southwest Virginia. There were no heels, no bright colors, no skin-tight pants. There were dreads and Birkenstocks and tie-dye t-shirts and baggy, earth-toned corduroys, and me. In my sexy, bright blue pants.

Discomfort and chagrin enveloped me. It quickly turned to dread. I debated running away before anyone I knew recognized me. But of course, as the only girl in neon blue pants, I had already been spotted. I reluctantly crossed the room and said hello to the few friends I had made, my eyes darting nervously and inquisitively around the party. I scanned the faces of each and every person (who were all certainly cooler than I was) for any look of judgment or disdain. Did I see those looks? Maybe, maybe not, but it didn't matter. Whether or not they existed, they existed in my head. Everyone there was judging me for my ridiculous outfit. Everyone there knew I was a fraud, and they were all sniggering behind my back.

So I did what any normal person would do after twenty minutes at a very uncomfortable party: I pretended to be sick and went home. In retrospect, it wasn't quite a lie. I was sick with embarrassment and sick of not knowing who I was. When I told Dan that I wasn't feeling well, he seemed genuinely concerned with my wellbeing. He wasn't scoffing at my outfit or anything else. Or was he? We weren't in high school anymore, right? But the damage was done. The lie was told. And I got back on the bus back to my dorm room and never wore those damn neon blue pants again.

That night is one of those shameful memories seared into my neural pathways; it will never leave me. Just because I was wearing the wrong fucking pants. I will remember every detail of walking into that party: the feeling of sinking dread as I saw how everyone was dressed and knew I had to keep walking through the door, utterly mortified, and the thoughts that ran through my head sitting alone on the bus on the way back to my dorm. I felt so stupid. I felt so torn. Was the girl in the blue pants the real me? Or was that just the person I created in Long Island? If all the things I had done were all part of an elaborate scheme to fit in, then where did that leave me when the new crowd wasn't anything like the ones before? I guess it was time to reinvent myself yet again.

I remained friends with those guys for a few months after that. I stopped wearing florescent pants and high heels, and I bought some cooler t-shirts because why didn't I have ANY cool t-shirts? We were friends, and they genuinely liked me, but I was still stuck in an endless cycle of trying to become whoever I wanted to befriend, unsure of any other way to do it. Imitation is the sincerest form of flattery, my mother would say.

As I grew through my years in college, I eventually grew into my own style. I stopped wearing things for other people, the feeling I felt at that party an ever-present reminder of the consequences of pretending to be too many different people. If you're wearing something for other people, and you end up around the wrong people, a chasm between your ought and actual selves will break open. That feeling of dread is the feeling that suddenly your actual self isn't aligning with who you think you're supposed to be in that moment, at that party, wherever. But if your ideal self is just wearing what you love, and your actual self is wearing what you love, then there can never be a gap between the two. Even if what you love is bright blue neon pants.

Back in April 2021, I was home in the U.S. staying at my mom's while I waited to get my second shot of the vaccine. I came downstairs one day wearing some big, baggy, very comfortable thrift-store overalls over a tiny, cropped Hooter's t-shirt that I found in the drawer of a dresser I also bought at a thrift store. The Hooter's motto reads, "Delightfully tacky, yet unrefined." The shirt is about the same size as a sports bra, and you could see the Māori tattoo that covers the left side of my torso. My mother looked at me, her brow furrowed, and the corners of her lips turned down in a blend of confusion and disdain, and said, "Honey, this is not how a thirty-seven-year-old lady dresses. You can see your tattoo! Maybe you want to go through my closet and pick out a few things?" She believed that 1). for some reason I would not want people to see a super-cool tattoo that I love, 2). that I was dressing this way just because I was too poor to afford nicer clothes, and 3). that I cared at all what a "thirty-seven-year-old lady" is supposed to dress like.

For the record, I thought this was a very cool outfit, and I was not just bumming around the house in it. But it offended her. She saw that outfit and was embarrassed *for* me. She wanted to donate some of her very expensive clothes to help me dress the way other women my age are supposed to dress. And if I did that, how would I feel? She would feel better seeing me rise up to the ought self she had created for me. And I would feel worse dressing like someone I'm not. When I explained to her that I actually liked my outfit, she looked even more upset and confused and replied, "Well, I hope you're not planning on wearing that to Mother's Day brunch."

No, mother. I am not planning on wearing a slutty Hooter's t-shirt and baggy overalls to Mother's Day brunch. I will wear a pretty floral skirt and blouse and take a shower and brush my hair. Because sometimes, getting dressed up is fun! Because you don't have to paint yourself into a single corner. You don't have to only always wear makeup or never wear makeup. You don't have to do anything. And putting on a pretty outfit for a nice Mother's Day brunch to go drink mimosas is a fun thing to do. Just like wearing a big hat to the Kentucky Derby or a ball gown to the opera!

Speaking of getting dressed up, remember how we stopped doing it for two years while we were all stuck at home? I think during lockdowns a part of all of us missed that special feeling when you just look *great*. When whatever you're wearing makes you feel so sexy and confident, and that charisma just exudes from your body as you walk down the street or smile coyly at a stranger. There is a lot to be said for that feeling.

But I think there is also a part of all of us that realized how wonderful it is to be comfortable. There will always be a place for that special date-night outfit. There will always be a time for heels and your little black dress. But one of the best things about spending more than a year at home in our pajamas is rethinking what we are willing to do for fashion. Why can't clothes be both cute and comfortable? Why do people only think I'm good at my job if I'm wearing a shirt cut in half with buttons down the middle? Why am I expected to wear heels TO WORK?

I used to wear fancy clothes. Really fancy clothes. As you are aware, I spent thousands and thousands of dollars that I didn't have on these clothes. I wore colorful five-inch heels and four-hundred-dollar sweaters paired with the perfect vintage skirt. I shopped at designer boutiques filled with gorgeous, unique things, and I paid no attention to the price tags. It was never really about the money; it wasn't about wearing labels. I needed those things to complete the picture of who I thought I wanted to become. I also had no real sense of the money I was spending either (thanks mom and dad), so there was that. It wasn't to impress other people necessarily (though that was always nice); it was to prove to myself that I was the woman I was trying to be. *Here is a well-dressed, edgy, fashionable, successful woman. Isn't she lovely! Look how great she looks in that Diane von Furstenberg. And what a chic-unique sense of style she has.* This was my ideal self that I wanted to project to the world. I needed the world to see it. If other people thought those things about me, then I was allowed to think them about myself. But I needed more and more new clothes each season to maintain it. I worked in finance and made good money but was drowning in debt from my ten-thousand-dollar-a-year projection of myself I had to maintain.

When I bought my one-way ticket to New Zealand (don't worry, we'll get into that), unsurprisingly, I didn't pack any four-hundred-dollar shoes. I got rid of all of the work clothes I loathed so intensely, I sold the designer bags my married ex-boyfriend bought me to help fund my trip, and I saved the beautiful items that I had collected and treasured for years in so many boxes in so many friends' closets up and down the east coast. Suddenly I had nothing but a single backpack with a few t-shirts, a couple of skirts, my favorite cotton dress (god, I miss that dress), a pair of corduroys, a pair of shorts, a hoodie, a cardigan, and of course, a beanie.

After that year abroad in New Zealand and Southeast

Asia living out of a backpack, I returned a changed woman. Not just because I had seen the world and tasted freedom for the first time in my life. It was also the first time I had visited a country where it was more socially acceptable to go barefoot than to wear high heels. There was something infinitely liberating about that. New Zealand was basically that hippie party in college, except this time I didn't show up in bright blue pants. Understanding that it didn't actually matter what I wore, understanding how much of this pressure was rooted in the schools I went to, the cities I had been living in, and the people I was surrounding myself with was life changing. It was a sudden realization that so much of what I cared about and based my decisions on was completely fabricated. It was a made-up world of bullshit that everyone else silently agreed to participate in. How come nobody told me?

To be abundantly clear, I don't not care about what I wear, all the contrary. Even after selling all my fancy clothes and escaping that life, I still have a personal sense of style. I still like to get dressed up from time to time. I have never, since I have grown into my own skin, been comfortable in an outfit that felt quiet or normal or expected. So I end up wearing seven different patterns with knee high socks over tights in the kind of fashion disaster that might end me up on a reality TV makeover show. Sideways glances abound at my slightly stained shirts covered in holes that are also eight years old. One of my friends used to call me "GAP Kids" because I was forever dressed like a twelve-year-old in a GAP Kids commercial. I know that what I wear says things about me, and I am totally okay with it. Some people probably think I look like a bum or that I look ridiculous. Other people probably think, *Damn, she really needs to brush her hair.* I don't care about those people. But hopefully some people are like, *Hey, that chick looks like she knows what's up.* And then I can go be friends with them.

I still care what I wear and still want people to think a certain thing when they see me. There is no escaping our own understanding of what our outer appearance represents. I'm no exception—no one is, except maybe the Dude.[12] The difference is that I don't care when they think the other things. I don't care if you think I look weird, maybe I think you look weird. Weird is relative, and there's no such thing as normal, so there's no point in trying to achieve it. As the famous French writer, designer, and filmmaker Jean Cocteau once said:

> *Style is a simple way of saying complicated things.*

There is nothing wrong with wanting to cultivate a look that defines you to the world, and there is nothing wrong with wanting to look and feel beautiful or edgy or raw or sweet or whatever mood you're in that day. But there is a dangerous line so many of us walk between what you're wearing because you love it and what you're wearing to project a particular image of yourself in order to garner the esteem of others. I felt terrible when I wore those blue pants because I had been wearing them for someone else. That version of myself was to please the people I had grown up with on Long Island. And because everything I was doing was for other people, I didn't make sense at that hippie party. All I wanted to do was be accepted rather than to be myself. There is absolutely nothing wrong with wearing neon blue pants at a party full of dirty hippies if that's who you are. And in all likelihood, half those hippies didn't give a shit about my pants.

Finding a balance between wearing clothes to live up to an idea of who you're supposed to be versus your authentic self isn't always easy. Our senses of style grow and change, sure, but they are still largely influenced by the places we live and the other strangers on the street we're surrounded by. I recently moved to Madrid where no one wears sweatpants to anywhere, and for the most part, women are incredibly well put together, with a bit of an edge to the aesthetic. They don't wear their hair in buns with

---

[12] Or Duder, or uh, El Dudarino, if you're not into the whole brevity thing.

no makeup and an old t-shirt from a festival, and they certainly don't wear Birkenstocks. When we first arrived, I thought okay, I live here now, I can adapt my sense of style into a more *Madrileña* vibe. It doesn't mean I'm not being me. Plus, I'm coming up on forty, maybe it's time I upgraded my wardrobe? Yeah, that idea lasted about three weeks. Why? Because as soon as I started trying to change the way I was dressing to make more sense in a new city, I felt like not me all over again. I felt like I was giving up a piece of myself to avoid the judgments (or garner the approval) of total strangers on the street.

No matter how confident you are in yourself, you can never exist in a vacuum from the societal norms and expectations that surround you. But what you can do is remember that it will always feel better to be yourself—once you accept that yourself is a valuable thing to be. If you've struggled with insecurity in the past, it's all too easy to let doubt creep back in. But don't let it. Let people think whatever they're going to think.

I want you to go through your closet and look at every item. Think about what projection of yourself it fits into. What ought self are you ascribing to when you wear these things? Think about the different places you might wear it. *This shirt is only for work, I would never be caught DEAD in that at the bar.* Put them all out on your bed into your different projections. *Here is "Work Taylor" and here is the "Fancy Taylor" and here is "Everyday Taylor" and here is the "Sexy Clubbing Taylor."* JK, I'm married and thirty-eight, I don't have clubbing tops. Okay, I have one. But that was certainly a large section of my closet in my twenties.

Look at all the projections of yourself and contemplate why one can't be the other. Why can't you be "everyday you" at the bar on Saturday night? How much do you feel like not yourself when you get dressed for work every day? My work clothes were like a prison jumpsuit that I would feverishly tear off the second

I got home. And when I realized how much I felt like not myself in those clothes, I realized how much I felt like not myself in my other clothes as well. I realized how much of what I was wearing was part of an elaborate show that had cost me thirty thousand dollars. I realized how much wearing high heels hurts your feet and who was I wearing them for anyway? So that a guy I flirt with at a bar can think my legs are longer than they are? Do my legs look much better in heels? Of course they do! Everyone's do. That's the whole point. But fuck that noise.

Eventually, I came to the conclusion that the real me is the one who goes to the grocery store and goes to the bar on a Tuesday and that person usually wears jeans and the same five t-shirts with her hair in a perpetual bun. Sometimes I wear cute dresses with funky patterns. Many of those patterns involve food for some inexplicable reason. All the time I wear whatever I feel like wearing. The most important piece here is to make sure nothing you're wearing is to garner approval or esteem from others. So if someone only approves of you or offers you esteem because you're dressed a certain way, then that person's approval is no longer valid nor desired.

One time back when I was single, a guy invited me out for a quick drink at a bar in the late afternoon. We weren't dating or anything, but looking back he was definitely trying to get in my pants. Whatever. I was wearing a somewhat grungy, crocheted hippie sweater and jeans with my hair in a bun, and I didn't feel like putting on a whole thing to go meet him, so I didn't. And when I got there—get this—he *forgave* me for looking so shitty. But since it was just this one time, and I normally kept it together, it was alright. Just this once. Get bent, Neil. If you know anyone like Neil, cut them out of your life immediately.

I want you to try wearing one of your projections of yourself in the wrong space. Wear your sexy going out clothes to the grocery store at ten a.m., or even better, wear your sweatpants to the club. You will probably feel awkward and out of place. You might feel like people are staring at you or saying things like, "Eww, why is that girl wearing sweatpants in this club?" You might feel invisible and overlooked when you're not getting the same level of attention. But if you're at a college bar in Wisconsin in winter, everyone will be wearing sweatpants, and you'll fit right in. At the grocery store you may feel like you're getting too much attention, that everyone is assuming you're on a walk of shame.

Whatever the situation you put yourself in, think through those thoughts and feelings carefully. Do they matter? Who are these people? Do you even care? Do you feel ashamed or liberated? One dangerous side effect of starting to wear whatever you want and not giving a fuck is that people will be intrigued by your confidence. *Who is this person who doesn't care? I wish I was that brave.* Of course, you're not brave. It's not scary to wear clothes. You should only really be scared of things that could potentially hurt you. And the slightly disdainful thoughts of strangers don't count as harm.

Let's say you decided to walk down the street in a garbage bag. Strangers would give you even weirder looks than your sweatpants in the bar. And then you would feel embarrassed, but why? You will never see these people again and, other than casually mentioning the garbage bag person they saw when they get home, they will never think of you again. So why do the opinions of complete strangers hold any weight in our decisions? Do you not wear a garbage bag because of what people will say? Because of what your friends would say? Or because garbage bags are ugly and uncomfortable, and it's cold outside? Hopefully, it's the latter of the three. Why do we allow our ideas of who we're supposed to be projecting at any given time, in any given place, affect our wellbeing—and even worse—our very happiness and sense of self-worth?

Take the different projections of yourself you got from your wardrobe. For each of these projections of yourself, there will be different reasons you ascribe to them:

1. I wear these clothes because I have to keep my job

2. I wear these clothes because they're comfy and I'm not going to be seen in public today

3. I wear these clothes because I want to look sexy/beautiful/attractive/whatever

4. I wear these clothes because I am going out in public but not to my job or to a place I am supposed to dress nicely

Most likely, those will be your four basic categories. Not everyone has to wear suits to work and not everyone cares about wearing sweatpants to the grocery store. That's totally fine. But if nobody cared, *would* you wear sweatpants to the grocery store? In a post-COVID world, maybe we already *are* wearing sweatpants to the grocery store. If nobody looked at you weird, would you wear low-cut sequined tops every day and thigh-high boots? Would you wear Joseph's technicolor dreamcoat and a pimp hat with a feather in it? Take every single article of clothing in your closet that you don't love wearing and put it aside. And then ask yourself, do I need this to keep my job? If so, sorry, but put it back for now. A girl gots to eat.

I want you to truly imagine a world where no one is around. You still have to go to the grocery store, you still go out to dinner, but there is no one there to judge you. What do you wear? For me, I like to wear grungy tops and high-waisted booty shorts and flat ankle boots. I like to wear multiple patterns at the same time. I wear those things when people are there, and I wear them when people are not. This is what I would wear on my imaginary, judgment-free planet. It is what I wear on our very real, judgment-filled planet. Soon, people will start telling me I'm too old to wear miniskirts and booty shorts (they already are, actually), and high-waisted things are out of style, and mom jeans are back in, and maybe they're right, but who gives a fuck? That's what I like. You heard me Gen Z, I'm keeping my high-waisted skinny jeans.

Find the thing that makes you feel the most like YOU when you wear it. Find the outfit that you feel comfortable and beautiful and sexy and cool in all the time. Not the outfit that gets you the girls at the bar or that dress that gets you so much attention every time you wear it. But the outfit that is the most you. Now look at all your other clothes and think how they relate to that version of you. That particular you that you most love to put out into the world, or maybe that you want to put out in the world but are too afraid to. And—here's the easy part—stop wearing anything that doesn't fit into that version of you. Like Marie Kondo says, throw out everything that doesn't spark joy.

If all of this has felt a little preachy and "be just like me," don't worry. You don't need to defy convention and conformity if that is the real you in there. *I love fancy clothes, and I love makeup, and I have plenty of money to spend on them, and that's the real me, and I don't wanna hear any different!* Fine. We're just trying to make sure the reasons behind what you're wearing and what you look like and all the other outer projections of yourself are coming from the right place. If you're getting older, and you're tired of dressing like a high schooler, upgrade that wardrobe. If you want to be taken more seriously at the office, I totes get it. You gotta do what you gotta do. If you love dressing like a Barbie doll with pink nails and high heels and fake eyelashes and cute little skirts, that's great; own it girl! Some people are probably going to perceive you as being shallow, or vapid, or superficial because that's what society has attached to that aesthetic. Fuck them. Prove them wrong. Wear. Whatever. The fuck. You want.

But if all of the clothes you love happen to be exactly the most expensive versions of clothes that are plastered across fashion magazines right now or what all of your sorority sisters are wearing—well, I don't believe you. Try a little harder. You have a unique voice; you have a unique style. I know this because everyone does. Everyone is moved by different kinds of art and music. Fashion is no different. When you're walking through a store, you see a dress or a shirt and think, *That's so me.* But then your bitchy friend laughed and said it was ugly, so you decided not to buy it. Whatever your perfect outfit and perfect music, wear it; listen to it; own it.

being yourself on purpose | 83

When you don't dress like everybody else, you don't have to think like everybody else.

—Iris Apfel

What we really want for ourselves is often and easily muffled by the noise of what we think other people want. So don't dress like everybody else. Don't think like everybody else. Don't spend money to buy the latest trends that will inevitably look weird and terrible in a year. And even weirder and more terrible-er in a decade. Don't buy the same belt or boots that ten thousand other girls are wearing right now. Wear whatever it is that makes you happy. Wear a grungy old shirt, wear crocs, wear a ten-thousand-dollar ball gown to the grocery store if you can afford it, I don't care. If you wear clothes that make you feel good, they can't go out of fashion. Because your style will forever be yours.

Bonus points: you will also save a shitload of money when you aren't in a race to keep up with the latest trends every season, reading fashion magazines to figure out what you're supposed to look like and how your hair is supposed to be cut. Real style is a confidence that you will never get from chasing seasonal ideas of what looks good.

Real style is never right or wrong. It's a matter of being yourself on purpose.

—G. Bruce Boyer

So be yourself. On purpose.

this is my f*cking face

If you're a woman and you wear makeup every day, you've probably had this experience. One day you're late for work or school or you just don't feel like it or you don't have the time to "put your face on"[13] and you get to wherever it is you're going and all the people who see you looking so fabulous in your makeup each and every day look at you with pitiful eyes, their heads slightly tilted to one side in some kind of feigned empathy and say, "Aww, you look tired today. Are you okay?"

You might answer something along the lines of, "Oh no, I just didn't have time to put my makeup on this morning."

The appropriate response, however, is:

I'm not tired. This is my fucking face.

This is a tough thing to write about because I know that so many women love makeup and wear it for themselves, and not to please other people, and just honestly prefer to look the way they look with makeup on. I get that. We all look better wearing makeup; that's the whole point. More power to you, etc., etc. But this is also a challenge. Because it's *hard* at first to stop. It's hard to just start walking around with everyone you know thinking you look really tired, and wondering if you have some personal problems, or assuming you picked up a drug addiction, or some

---

[13.] I hate this phrase, by the way, and let's all agree to never use it again.

other nefarious rumors they've started in their own heads. It's also hard to be walking down the street next to a hundred other women who clearly spent two hours getting ready in the bathroom and being like, *Welp, guess I will never be considered attractive again.* So here is the lesson I'm trying to impart, and please, prepare yourself for the cliché. You ARE still beautiful. People WILL still find you attractive (including yourself). And it will take some time before you can truly see your face again for what it is: you.

I lost my makeup habit when I started traveling in New Zealand. Shocker, I know. Backpackers don't carry a lot of beauty products, and there just wasn't a pressure to be wearing it because no one else was either. Then I started traveling in Southeast Asia. And to be sure, there is way less of a beauty regimen standard among travelers there. Everyone is just traveling. Some girls still wear the basic eyeliner and mascara, some real fancy chicks may even wear eyeshadow, but it just doesn't matter. And it honestly felt silly in the face of all the awe-inspiring things I was doing and all the beautiful local people I was seeing many of whom were, coincidentally, not wearing makeup.

Traveling has an intoxicating ability to melt away all the things that don't really matter. Because of that fact it ends up distilling the things that do. And what traveling did for me, perhaps a year of coronavirus quarantine has done for so many others. We are emerging from our homes and back into a whole new world with a renewed questioning into what really matters. Maybe we have finally gotten used to seeing our faces just a bit more naturally, and maybe it isn't so bad after all?[14]

While this rant is not an insistence that you stop wearing makeup because you're not being true to yourself, it is a plea that you take a moment to think about why you do.

What if you wore your normal makeup one day, but no

[14.] Then again, plastic surgery rates have also gone up because everyone's been staring at their imperfections in Zoom calls for two years, so perhaps my pleas to accept your face as-is are falling on deaf, yet perfectly reconstructed, ears.

one had told you that makeup had completely changed overnight. We now wear huge purple circles around our eyes and blue polka dots on our lips. Your makeup looked flawless when you looked in the mirror, but now everyone is staring. You can see that what you are wearing on your face is now making you less attractive to everyone on the street. Does it still make you feel good? Or now do you feel silly? I'm sure many of you still wouldn't give a fuck, in which case, carry on. But the point is that beauty is subjective; it changes with time. And more importantly, it changes from culture to culture. Nothing that you think is objectively attractive, is.

Remember that experiment a few years ago where a lady sent a photo around to eighteen different countries asking for them to make her "beautiful" in Photoshop, and of course, eighteen very different photos came back? Being tan is avoided at all costs in Asia, being too skinny is unattractive in Colombia, and of course the American model had to have a thigh gap. In the nineties she needed to be a waif like Kate Moss, now she needs to be thicc. I read somewhere recently that "asses are getting replaced by breasts again." So I guess now ass implants are out and boob jobs are back? Who on god's green earth writes this shit?

Our makeup routines change with each generation, with each pendulum swing of style in one direction or the other, until we're reading Buzzfeed articles entitled "20 Embarrassing Makeup Trends Every 00s Girl Remembers" and cringing at the sparkly blue eyeshadow we used to so liberally apply. Gen Z TikTok'ers are literally drawing dark circles under their eyes (seriously, wtf?). But what if you didn't have to cringe when you looked back in a photo and you didn't have to wonder why anyone ever thought crimping their hair was a good idea?

Take a moment to think about how much time it takes you to put on your makeup each day. Now take a separate moment to think about how much it costs you. No seriously, actually add it up. I tried to buy some foundation for a Halloween costume last year and almost fainted at the price and then totally wore a different Halloween costume that didn't involve spending seventeen dollars on makeup I will never wear again. Now take a moment to think about what would happen at your job if you showed up wearing nothing but your (GASP!) face. Just your face. The way it looks all the time. That one you were born with. I never wore a lot of makeup to begin with—just eyeliner, eyeshadow, mascara—and I still have the same stick of eyeliner from 2011 that I use three or four times a year. I know it makes me look better. I'm not denying that. I wear it when I have an event to go to or when I go on a date with my husband. I wear it when I want to feel a little sexier than normal. But my biggest problem with the daily application of makeup by ninety-nine percent of women is that we've all agreed to get in on this lie. We've made it so that natural beauty means "wearing less makeup." We've made it so that we're all ashamed of our faces and we come out screaming on social media: *I wear makeup for me! Not for any man!*

Because you want to look more beautiful. Because the face you already have isn't beautiful enough. Whether you're doing that for you or for someone else, does it really matter? Isn't it essentially the same concept: here is a way to make myself look better because the way I already look isn't good enough for me or for anyone else? Seriously, why are men allowed to just wear their fucking faces around and women aren't?

The last point I will make on the topic is one that I sometimes struggle with as a woman on a freight train straight to irrelevance: aging. Women are not allowed to age. We are not supposed to age. Wrinkles are the enemy, and we will spend thousands of dollars on Botox and skin creams and anything else to stop the process. And we can get right back into these arguments about *I do it for myself, and it gives me confidence.* Regardless of your reasons, there is something that's wholly unnatural about stopping your body from going through this inevitable cycle of life or pretending it isn't. We're going to age. Whether you look sixty at the age of sixty or at the age of forty or eighty, you're still going to be old. And being old is spectacular. Because you finally don't have to care what anyone thinks of you anymore! Because you've learned to embrace your body and your wrinkles and your stretch marks and all of your imperfections. Every scar and age spot and crow's foot is part of your miraculous decades upon decades of life on this planet! Because you've stopped giving a fuck. Because you're old enough to know the difference between what truly matters and what doesn't.

    I recently learned that there is a term for this: it's called body neutrality. The whole body positivity movement is a little toxic if you ask me. Telling women that they should think their stretch marks and their fat rolls and their acne are beautiful is disingenuous at best, and damaging at worst. So no, you don't have to think your acne is beautiful or that your un-made-up face looks equally as attractive as your made-up face. What you have to realize is that your value in this world should have absolutely nothing to do with how beautiful or not beautiful society has deemed your face to be.

    Makeup makes us all more attractive by conventional standards, sure. But what's so wrong with just being as attractive as you already are? How about we start looking for value in more valuable places?

#blessed

Social media, of course, presents us with exactly the opposite idea. It tells us that happy people are pretty and have fun, pretty friends, and interesting jobs, and do yoga, #choosejoy #blessed. It tells us the best way to dress and the best food to eat. Everyone is walking around this crazy planet trying to figure out how to get to this elusive *happy* and Instagram influencers are here to show us how it's done. Just because these are the ways we are most frequently presented with happiness doesn't remotely mean they are the only paths to find it. It also doesn't mean people on Instagram who look happy are happy at all.

It's no secret that people don't post their shitty days on Instagram or Facebook (does anyone even post anything on Facebook anymore?). Even the hashtag, #iwokeuplikethis is full of doctored pictures and people pretending to pass off their made-up faces as candid, natural beauty. People take fake pictures of themselves sleeping with "their bae" (I know I'm old, and no one says this anymore, but I started writing this book in 2017) and fake pictures pretending they're at the beach or on a spectacular vacation. We see #vanlife Instagrammers living a hobo-chic dream with pictures of sexy blondes doing yoga through their open van door overlooking a coastal sunrise. But it took forty-seven shots to get that photo, and they spend their days missing out on real experiences because they are too busy cultivating fake ones for money.[15]

---

[15]. Check out the Instagram @influencersinthewild for a good laugh.

I'm not saying they're not happy, maybe they are. But creating an enviable life is exactly what they're being paid by marketers to do. Instagram's entire business model is built on envy. When you remember that those vanlifers don't even have their own place to poop, maybe #vanlife seems a little less glamorous.

Maybe you have seen some Instagrams of digital nomads or travel bloggers or whoever else lying in a hammock with a laptop and a cocktail with the caption, "this is my office today #digitalnomad #lifeisgood #blessed" or whatever other hashtags they use. Again, just because this seems like the perfect life, it isn't. It's lonely and hard traveling all the time. The money is volatile, and you're constantly meeting people and saying goodbye. Sure, it can seem glamorous, but most things about traveling are decidedly unglamorous. Then again, maybe you would love it. Maybe you should make the switch to remote work and never go back to your office again. Just stop basing your goals and your dreams on Instagram. Stop wishing you were skinnier or had better hair. By the way, I totally wish I had better hair, but I've come to terms with the limp, paper-thin, tangled bird's nest that sits atop my head. It's one of those things I can't change anyway, so why waste my time and energy and money fighting it?

Happiness isn't a great job. It isn't great hair. Happiness isn't being friends with the cool kids. Seeing what you imagine to be the most successful, happy people, and emulating them, is not the way to achieve happiness for yourself. I know, I tried it. Trying to adopt someone else's idea of happiness or making your life look like anyone else's in order to find it for yourself is the surest way to never achieve it.

If you had all the money and all the clothes and the perfect hair and the perfect car, what would you have? And I don't mean perfect according to Instagram, but perfect according to you. If you finally cultivated exactly the perception you were going for, and you put it out there in the world, what would you get in return? What's the payoff? Adoration? Respect? A hot girlfriend? The perfect girlfriend? Money? Fame? This is how we answer the question of authenticity versus perception. If there is an answer to that question, then your choices, your clothes, your anything is based in external esteem and perception. If the answer to that question is: I would feel satisfied with myself, and I would feel like my outsides were matching the person on the inside, then you're on the right track.

But we still have some peeling to do.

the happiness inventory

Thus far, the concept of "living your authentic life" or "doing whatever the fuck you want" has been admittedly vague. So, I shouldn't wear clothes to impress other people, but do I have to quit my job and move to New Zealand? Do I have to sell all my belongings? Do I have to become a hippie and live in a van down by the river? What if I don't wanna travel? And if I don't care about what society expects of me can I still work in a cubicle and come home to my apartment covered in decorative pillows that say *Live, Laugh, Love!*?

Sure! I'm not here to tell you what to do. That's the whole beauty of this way of life. There are varying degrees of saying "fuck it," and not everyone has to quit their job, get dumped, sell everything they own, and travel the world. That was just my schtick. That being said, it's more than likely that if you are reading this, you want to make a change bigger than your throw pillows.[16] So how do we figure out what we really want?

As we have already discussed, the traditional path for most people involves going to college, getting a job, getting an apartment, and eventually getting married and then usually having babies. We upgrade from an apartment to a bigger house. We

---

[16.] If the #1 change you're looking for is more money, I can recommend some very different books for you to read. But then put this one down right now. I'm not saying you can't be rich AND happy, but the lessons I have to offer are for those of us who aren't searching for "the American dream," but rather for a new brand of happiness. What are you doing still reading? I told you to put this fucking book down.

move to the suburbs and then . . . that's it. This is the correct linear progression of adulthood that has been prescribed for us. But living in the same house in the same place at the same job for however many years is the easiest way to forget why you do what you do, or how you got there in the first place. We occupy ourselves with daily trivialities, slowly filling our spaces with more things than we need without ever stopping to ask, *Why?* Or, *Do I even want this?* We create things to worry about and occupy our thoughts, like who gets the next rose on *The Bachelor,* or how that prick cut me off in traffic, or why Linda was such a bitch yesterday.

It's the easiest thing to get to this place. I think most of the developed world is in this place. You just forget to take stock of your life for long enough that you can't count the inventory anymore. But it's also never too late to do it, no matter how overcrowded the stock room is.

Think about your life as it is, right now, in its entirety. Think about your house or apartment, your car, your bicycle, your cat, the dishes in your cupboards, how full your dirty laundry basket is. Think about your habits, your routines, the TV shows you watch, the meals you cook, your gym membership. Think about the friends you see regularly, the ones you don't, and the places you go each week.

Now think about how happy each of those things makes you. How many of them contribute meaningfully to your happiness each and every day? How many of them do you want to change? How many could you live without? How many do you truly hate? We need to Marie Kondo not just our stuff, but our relationships and habits as well. How many of the things and people that occupy your life truly bring you joy?

What about your job, your office, your boss, your average work week? Do you like it? Are you happy going to work? And I don't mean ecstatic, over-the-moon happy—everyone begrudges work to some degree. That's why they call it work. Let's phrase it a different way. Have you ever been driving to work, sitting in traffic, and thought:

What if I just got in an accident? Not a big one, nothing serious. But just serious enough to put me in the hospital for a few days . . . maybe just a broken leg . . . man, wouldn't that vacation be nice?

If you haven't thought about crashing your car to get out of work (and I certainly did), good for you! It's not as bad as I thought.[17]

Now, take your inventory of all those things you do and own that make you happy or unhappy and make a list. Make a list of the worst things in your life, the things that cause you the most frustration. *My boyfriend never listens to me. My job sucks. I want to try new things, but I'm scared. My mom is sick. I'm too fat. I work too many hours. I'm broke. I have too much anxiety. I don't have nice clothes.*

Write down all the best things in your life: *I live close to the beach. I have really good friends. I'm a good painter. My butt looks awesome in these jeans.* It doesn't matter what it is, if you have a feeling about it, write it down.

Lastly, make a list of all the things you want in your life. *I want a Range Rover. I want a sexier boyfriend. I wish I could move to Paris. I want to stop worrying about how fast my windshield wipers are wiping,* whatever.

As you write down each negative thought, positive thought, and desire, consider what kind of thought each one is. Is this the kind of problem you can fix? If your boyfriend is a dick, then yes. You can leave him. If your mom is sick, then I'm sorry, that sucks, but you can't fix it. But you can fix how you feel about it and how it affects you. If you're listing things that seem to be rooted in an external concept of success such as, *I want nicer clothes*, or *I want to get a raise,* I will tell you right now, fixing them won't make you feel any better. Okay, so getting a raise can make a huge difference in a lot of people's lives in a country where even double the minimum wage means hovering dangerously close

---

[17]. My editor told me upon reading this that a friend of his fantasizes the bank she works at will just burn down one day, so I know I'm not alone here.

to poverty, and basically no one can afford their rent anymore. You are allowed to both want and demand a raise. But for those who are already financially stable, a raise may make you feel successful and accomplished for a minute, but it won't ever truly make you happy. Buying more expensive clothes will never fix your low self-esteem.

Look over your list and break each of those desires down to the root. I want to get a raise because _____. Because why? If it's so you can feed your family or finally afford a fucking vacation, then you get to keep that on the list. And it's time to start thinking about what you can do to make that goal happen.

But if it's for literally anything other than your basic physiological and psychological needs, you don't need it. And beyond that, it won't work. *I want to get a raise so I can get a bigger apartment.* Why? What's the apartment going to provide for you that your current apartment isn't? A nicer balcony? A bigger closet? You seem to be doing just fine. *I want nicer clothes because all my clothes are out of fashion.* So? Who the fuck cares? *I want new clothes because all mine have holes in them, and I'm tired of looking like a bum.* Okay, now we're getting somewhere. Only hobos like me wear clothes filled with holes. And even I want new clothes from time to time.

If looking nicer will make you truly feel better about yourself—if it will help your actual self align with your authentic, ideal self and provide internal rather than external esteem—then it's valid. But I promise you don't need seven-hundred-dollar shoes to do it. Whenever any of our desires in life are in order to get us to the "next level" or satisfy a secondary, external desire (like esteem from our friends or strangers), they are misguided, and they usually won't satisfy you in any meaningful way. Leaving a job you hate and escaping a shitty relationship, on the other hand, can make you feel better. There is no secret solution here: do as many things that bring you joy and as few things that don't.

So you've got your list of the things that make you happy and unhappy and things to stop doing and start doing. How many of the complaints on your list are things you can't change?

I wish I was taller. Cross them off. How many of those things are based on money or material possessions? How many are based on external sources of approval or acceptance? Cross them all off. I know it still seems like having a perfect wardrobe or driving a fancy car would solve your problems, but it won't. Ever. If you want those things to impress your friends or people you're dating, then you're going to be attracting people who don't want you for who you are. If you only think your girlfriend is pretty with makeup on, you don't love her (sorry). If you wouldn't be dating your boyfriend if he didn't have such a nice car (or you wish he had a nicer car because you're embarrassed to be seen in his 1998 hatchback), you don't really love him either. If you won ten million dollars in the lottery today, would you stay with your current partner? If not, then it's time to leave, with or without the ten million. We'll talk more about deriving internal esteem from money and material possessions in a bit, but for now, cross it off.

Okay, so how is your list? Now that we have crossed off everything that we want that is based in money, and everything we want because it will impress someone else, and everything that we cannot control, we should have a list of things that are actually attainable and will have a positive impact on our lives. We should have a list of things we can do, and that we can make happen, but for whatever reason, we just haven't yet, like losing ten pounds, or trying new restaurants, or just moving to fucking Paris already. Whether it's fear, or laziness, or fitting in, there is a reason you haven't made the choice to do these things yet. Maybe your list looks something like this:

> *I want to have more friends*
> *I want a girlfriend*
> *I want to write a book*
> *I want to travel for a year*
> *I want to start playing a sport*
> *I want to do more things on the weekend*
> *I want to be less judgmental*

> *I want to watch less TV*
> *I want to stop hanging out with Linda*
> *I want to care less what people think about me*

Great job! Now how many things on your list are low-hanging fruit: things you don't like to do with people you don't really want to be friends with? How many things could you theoretically stop or start doing this very moment? Watch less TV, start playing a sport, exercise more, watch more TV, do more on the weekends, stop hanging out with fucking Linda. What's stopping you from doing any of those things? Nothing. That's why these are the low-hanging fruit. They are those tiny choices you can make right now, every day. Right before you turn the TV on, in that one second before you hit the power button, when your brain reminds you that you said you didn't want to do it—listen. Don't turn it on. Read a book, or take a bike ride or a walk, or cook something, or ask someone if they want to hang out. It doesn't matter. As long as it's not fucking Linda.

Remove as many negative influences from your life as possible and fill your life with things you love. I know, it sounds super obvious. Yet somehow, we get stuck in these lives that don't fulfill us. We fill our voids with TV and shopping and pass the time until the next weekend comes around. We stay in unhealthy relationships because we're afraid to be alone. We marry the wrong guy because he was there at the right time. I promise, it's okay to stop being friends with people who don't add anything positive to your life. Cut ties with people who make you feel small and people who make you feel like *not* you. If you act a certain way around one friend and a different way around another, then one of those roles you're playing isn't real. Figure out which one makes you feel worse, and walk away. If you don't like going to yoga, stop going to yoga.

If you're feeling stuck because you want to do more things, but you never have friends to do things with, then just do the things. Literally. I know it sounds scary and going places alone makes you a weirdo, but it really doesn't. You just go. You can go to a museum alone; you can go to the movies alone. You can go on a hike, on a trip, to a restaurant. You can move to fucking New Zealand alone. The only place this fear comes from is your own fear of failure or what other people would think. Let that sink in. You're not doing something you want to do because of what complete strangers would think while you're doing it, or what you would think about yourself, which is even weirder, cause you're you! You can give yourself permission to do anything. And the silliest part of all is, strangers don't care what you do! They didn't care when you wore a garbage bag down the street, and they don't care you're eating alone. No one sees a guy reading a book at a café and thinks, *What a loser, doesn't he have any friends?*

When I was traveling on my own, I never got one hundred percent used to eating alone. It still felt awkward sometimes, and I was always in and out pretty fast. But why did I feel that way? Why was it awkward? Did anyone in the restaurant care I was alone? No. That is one hundred percent in my head. The sooner you realize how little other people care what you do—and that their opinions don't matter even if they do—the sooner you can start doing whatever the fuck you want.

If you love staying at home and playing video games and don't like exercise, then don't fucking exercise. I don't exercise because I hate it, and it makes me miserable, and I don't care that all my friends keep telling me how great yoga will make me feel. I've tried it; I'm not that into it. As Joan Rivers once said, "The day I see a runner smiling, I'll consider it." If I cared about being healthy, I wouldn't smoke half a pack a day. What I'm saying is, the list above shouldn't be your list. Maybe an item on your list is, *I want to feel less guilty for playing so many video games,* and that's okay too. Video games are awesome. If your ought self is telling you that successful grownups don't play video games and that's why you need to stop, then tell your ought self to get bent. Your ideal self should be the happiest version of yourself. And if video games make you happy, then keep fucking playing video games.

Each of these micro-decisions we make every day, these paint the picture of who we are. Not our jobs or our houses or our degrees, or lack thereof. You have to strip out the choices you're making to appease your ought self and the habits you've created to silence the void between actual and ideal. When you start making these micro-decisions in line with what will bring happiness into your own life, you're finally being true to the real you. We have to shift our ideal selves in order for this to work, or we will continue to try to work toward an outdated ideal, an ideal that is clouded with the voices of our ought selves.

Once you have immediately done everything on your list that is immediately doable . . . what's that? It's not that easy to just stop answering Linda's calls? Of course it is. Because you want it. Because you wrote this down as a part of your life that was making you unhappy. You thought of everything that you do, and Linda came up as a negative influence. Tell her why; maybe it will help her come to terms with some of her own shit.

Once you realize that the reason you aren't doing these things is because you're scared of change, or scared of failure, or because people will think you're weird, then you can just do them. Because those aren't real reasons. People think everyone is weird, who cares? Change isn't scary; it's just different. Failure is only scary if we're talking about your parachute failing after you jump out of an airplane. No matter what you do or try or fail at, there will always be something on the other side. Things will always be okay as long as you're okay with them being whatever they are.

It should go without saying at this point, but I'll offer you a reminder nonetheless: if any of the things on your list are based on something you have seen somewhere else or some idea of what a great, sexy, successful person is, take them off. If you want to lose ten pounds because you just want to get healthier and you're tired of being a lazy, pizza-eating sack of shit, then great. But if you love being a lazy, pizza-eating sack of shit (I know I do), then ask yourself who you're losing the ten pounds for? There is no right or wrong answer to the things that you want to do. There are only right and wrong reasons. And for everything you think is wrong with you or needs to be changed because it doesn't fit into society's ideals, there is someone else out there who has/loves/wants that same thing. If the internet has taught us anything, it's that no matter how deviant from the supposed norm your interests are, there's someone else out there with the same crazy fetish.

The sooner you realize that you can never be satisfied chasing someone else's idea of happiness, the sooner you can be satisfied with who you really are. Even if that person is a chubby, pizza-eating, yoga-hating cynic. Just don't be mean to other people.

what would you say you do here?

It may be easy to change the things we do in our free time, but changing jobs or careers isn't nearly as easy, right? We all need money to eat and live and pay our rent and stuff. I get it.

But, if you hate the job you have right now, here's a real crazy question for you . . . do you already know the other thing you want to do? If you do, congratu-fucking-lations because you're way ahead of the game. If you always wanted to dance or write a book or you're interested in graphic design, or whatever, you can just do it. Go back to school at night. Start doing it on weekends. Take a class, build up a side business; there are a million different resources on how to do this in almost any field.

Nola Ochs started college in 1930, quit, got married, had an entire family, and then went back and graduated college at the age of ninety-five. And then she went on to become a storyteller on a cruise ship because apparently that's an actual job title. What's your excuse? I don't care if you've been an event planner for thirty years, and you hate it; I promise you can still do something else.

Or maybe you just hate your job because your company culture is toxic, or you sit right next to fucking Linda. Then start looking for moves to other companies in your industry. Like now. Even if that other job is in Akron, Ohio or Daytona Beach or Paris-fucking-France. You can move, I promise. And the absolute worst thing that could happen is that you hate the new place you moved to, and then you wouldn't even be any worse off since you already hate where you are!

Or maybe your problem right now is that you're stuck in a job you hate but have no idea what else you would even do. My answer to that is try some things out. Apply for jobs you don't even think you could get. Work at a bar on a weekend and see if you like it (most people enjoy it for a couple years before the intolerable cruelty of punishing hours and terrible humans starts to break them down). Hate waiting tables? The internet is a miraculous place. Start exploring. Maybe you want to start a YouTube channel on knitting or write a blog or literally fucking anything—it's the internet. You can teach English to kids in China; you can sell pictures of your feet to dudes with a foot fetish for fuck's sake. There is absolutely no reason in 2022 to be stuck in a job you hate on a path to a career you're not even sure you want, even if it's a career you've been in for twenty years.

Now I have an even bigger secret: even if you can't quit your job that you hate (I still think you can, but let's just say you really can't) it doesn't mean you're destined to a life of unhappiness. You can work in a desk job that you don't care about at all or flip burgers or clean toilets or whatever else and leave it behind at the end of day. You can work in a positive, supportive environment where you are personally and professionally valued—even if that job is data entry or bartending. And when you go home at the end of the day you have plenty of hours to devote to building model trains, or knitting, or cooking, or playing video games, or whatever else it is that you actually like to do. You don't have to leave your job to pursue your passion if you can find happiness doing both. And you definitely don't have to pin your esteem and happiness on a career in the first place.

On the flip side, you could land what you think is your dream job in your dream field only to feel marginalized and creatively stifled. Your boss undercuts your work and micromanages you; your colleagues are toxic ladder-climbers willing to throw any- and everyone under the bus. Fuck that place; get out as fast as you can. In my case, I have been able to write books for the last few years . . . huzzah! I should be at one with the world! All my dreams have come true! But, as it turns out, reading and

what would you say you do here? | 103

writing for money means I haven't done any of my own writing. My travel blog is years behind, and my journals sit empty next to my bed. When you read all day for work, you no longer feel like reading a book at the beach or on the weekend. Sometimes, when the thing you love doing becomes your job, it turns it into work, go figure. Working in a field you're passionate about is not a guarantee for job satisfaction or a recipe for happiness. No job is a recipe for happiness.

Comics about work. Made with love & lots of coffee.
Join r/workchronicles or follow on Instagram/Twitter/FB

Work Chronicles
workchronicles.com

And seriously, who is happy at work? Who created this myth? Our capitalist overlords? As Americans, we work longer hours and take fewer vacations than almost any country in the world . . . why? Because we love delivering profits to CEOs and shareholders? Actually, yes. It's because you've been told this has value by society. Being too busy is a badge of honor, every hobby should be turned into a side hustle, and if you work the minimum amount possible just to get by, you're deemed a lazy piece of shit. They somehow convinced us that our jobs should define our whole existence so that we devote every ounce of ourselves to them rather than pursuing our own happiness. They convinced us that the more monetary value we produce, the more value we have as humans. They mindfucked us all into thinking a job should actually be a dream that we have! Damn they're good.

 I don't know about you, but my personal dream is to be a trust fund baby and travel the world indefinitely, forever staying as long as I want in each country, writing random books that would never sell like *The Casual Geologist*. But, since I have to eat, I continue to take jobs that are not something I dream about ever. I take jobs that pay my bills without sacrificing my minimum requirements for employment: I have to be able to work from home, have a flexible schedule, and my employer must be comfortable with my current LinkedIn photo, which is a picture of me in a tank top with a beer in Cartagena trying to shove an entire fish in my mouth. As long as employers aren't trying to shove their expectations down my throat about how many tattoos signify that I can't be trusted with a client, I'm happy to do work I'm not passionate about (the answer in finance, by the way, is any).

 I'm happy to make less money to have the freedom that I've realized is most important to me. I fucking hate marketing and social media, but I did it for years. I still do it. I've cleaned toilets and made beds and worked in bars and conducted phone interviews and done data entry. I've lived at the poverty line, and I've lived above the median. These days I'm swinging dangerously close to the former. As long as the jobs supported me, it didn't matter that I wasn't a famous author living off my royalties. Because I didn't tie my happiness to my career, my career didn't get to determine my happiness.

 There was a time while I was living in New Zealand, after I had traveled around Southeast Asia for four months, when I was utterly and completely broke. I had zero dollars to my name. There was no credit card to max out, no mom to bail me out. I couldn't get a job; I even tried waiting tables at a strip club in Wellington (surprise, they really just want you to strip). Eventually, I ended up getting a job at a hostel in a tiny town on the South Island called Wanaka. I had to borrow money from a friend just to get the bus down there. Here is where I began my illustrious toilet-cleaning career.

My meager income paid for the bed in the shared dorm room I lived in, and not much else. I lived off the free food that backpackers left in the hostel refrigerator, and I collected spare change I found on the sidewalk. Literally. One day, my only shoes were stolen from the hostel and—I shit you not—for two weeks of my life, I didn't own shoes. It's surprisingly un-weird to walk around New Zealand barefoot. I had no friends, no money, and no fucking shoes. I was desperately lonely. As incredible as travel is, you are going to be sad. You are going to be lonely. Hopefully you will always have shoes.

And yet somehow, Wanaka ended up becoming my favorite place in the world. I got a second job slinging pizzas and made some life-long friends. We lived a simple life, drinking beers by the lake or going on hikes, and that was it. I had moved the goal posts about what it meant to be happy. I learned that you can be happy with so very little. It didn't have to be traveling and exploring new places and seeing new things; it didn't even have to be writing. It could just be existing in a beautiful place with good people, even with a relatively (and literally) shitty job. I was still getting to live the life I wanted without sacrificing a single part of who I am. Did cleaning toilets suck? Of course it did, they're fucking toilets—in a hostel. But every minute I wasn't cleaning toilets, I was living in a beautiful town with wonderful people.

I promise you there is a life where your job is a means to an end and not the defining factor of your identity. There is a world where you go in, do your work, and then spend the rest of your time doing whatever it is you love. We don't have to be defined by what we do for money. We absolutely shouldn't be defined by what we do for money. If what you love and what makes you money overlap, great. Deriving internal and external esteem from being totally awesome at your job are both completely valid forms of esteem. If you love your job and you're great at it, more power to you! If not, who the fuck cares?

Somehow, despite the fact that the majority of people work in jobs so they can eat and pay rent—and not because they're super passionate about marketing or waiting tables—our careers have become an inextricable part of our identities in the modern world. The first question to roll from the lips of a mingler at any cocktail party is inevitably, "So, what do you do?" Why don't we instead start asking people "So what do you do for fun?" We should be defined by what we enjoy doing and what we choose to spend our time on. We should be defined by the way we treat other human beings. If you're worried about what people might think when you tell them you work at a gas station or as a garbage man, just remember: other people's thoughts on what you do, or why, or what you enjoy don't matter. Don't let them.

You can quit your job, I promise. You can be happier, I promise. You can separate your self-worth from your career success, I promise. Listen to your self-guide for a minute. It's there to tell you where you want to go.

february 2011

    Sitting outside at the bar of a hotel we could never afford to stay in, I crack a joke of a smile and deeply inhale the last drag of my cigarette. A tear flips salty over my lip, a single escapee from the wells of my glossy eyes. My flight from Christchurch to Sydney to Los Angeles to Washington, DC is leaving at five a.m., a mere seventeen hours away. Kirra and I order a second round of boozy coffees. Everything I have loved for the last four months exists here. Everything I have come to learn about myself in the past year was solidified here. And now I am heading back to a place with which I feel distantly disconnected. A biological parent I have never met. America is a part of me and always will be. But the home I now know lies elsewhere. It lies in the tiny traveler's town of Wanaka nestled on the southern shore of the lake that shares its name. It lies in the yellowed, tomato-toned hair of the best friend I have made here. It lies in the torn, ratty clothes filling the backpack in the back of our beat-up van.

    But there is nothing to be done. For all my spontaneity, all my reckless whims, this flight is leaving, and I have to be on it. My working visa is expired. My attempts at a student visa failed with a swift certainty that assured me I was not meant to stay in New Zealand. I have less than $1,000NZ and much of that has been promised to my mother who has been dutifully paying the student loans on which she unfortunately co-signed all those years ago. I have to go back. Kirra and I spend the night getting drunk with one of our favorite couchsurfers with whom we happened to cross paths again. We pretend it is not my last night. I am a terrible liar. When two a.m. rolls around, the jig is up. We make our way back to the hostel to finish packing everything I can ever remember owning.

    At four thirty in the morning, I stumble bourbon drunk through Kiwi customs with a moldy passport, a backpack stuffed tighter than a Vietnamese bus, and my trusty messenger bag, still caked in the dried clay from slippery, scarring Cambodian roads. Shaking his head at a sight he probably too often sees, the customs officer puts up a sham of an objection to my taped-together state before finally letting me through to the gate. I used every shred of energy I had to hold the pieces together, to get stamped and get to the other side. And now, sitting outside the gate in the unquestionable pre-dawn dark, I turn up my music to drown out the water-logged heaves of my own heavy heart. There is no running now.

Coming home is like going back in time. Nothing has changed, save for a new CVS there, a different bar on the corner. I return to the mess I left strewn up and down the eastern seaboard in the wake of my sudden departure. Four years of clothes and furniture and books and movies and art and crap are waiting to be collected, to be sold, to be thrown away. And for the first time in my life, I don't want them. Sorting through the bags of four-hundred-dollar shoes and thousand-dollar dresses, it all seems so silly to me. I see thirty thousand dollars of debt sewn imperceptibly into each delicate thread. You don't realize how little you can live on until you leave it behind. The things I coveted, the life and apartment I spent so many years building are nothing but dust. The worst part is, they always were; I am only now just seeing it. Suddenly I am drowning in these over-washed masses.

There was bound to be culture shock coming home to the land of the overworked, of fast food and gratuitous shoes. But I have a plan. Sell as much of my stuff as I can. Give away the rest. Get a job teaching English in South Korea. They will pay for my flight. Home in February, gone by June. I will not get stuck here. I will not buy a pair of shoes. I will not let this place take it from me twice.

But what to me is a life changing revelation is nothing but crazed words from a dirty hippie to the rest of the workaday world. After all, who in metropolitan America takes advice from a greasy-haired barefooted girl? Something in me expects the universe to react to my changed soul. As if I were the first to discover it and the sheer energy of what I have unlocked inside me would alert the population, "Wake up! The time has come, this is no longer the life you have to lead!" But life is always only routine, and most people cower at the threat of change. Shake the world and they will cling to whatever is nailed to the ground.

I make less sense here than I ever did before.

moving the goal posts

Hopefully at this point you're doing fewer things that make you miserable and fewer things to appease your ought self. Hopefully you're getting closer to understanding who your ideal self really is. Maybe you're pondering your job and coming to terms with whether or not you wanna do it for the rest of your life. Maybe you understand a little more about why you dress the way you do or why you spend money on the things you do. Most people probably already know their personal style, and that's wonderful. But I think far too many people spend far too much money trying to cultivate that style in order to garner esteem, which makes them feel poor, which makes them feel inadequate or insecure and leads to lots more anxieties, and ironically, lower self-esteem.

As part of the deal living in a capitalist society, money is unquestionably the ultimate indicator of success. We want good jobs so we can get paid more money so we can have nicer things to show off how successful we are. We all want nice things, even a poor bum like me. The issue arises when those *things* become the end in themselves; they become a part of your ought self and your ideal self and drive the decisions you make every day.

When your own personal concept of success and esteem and your own life goals are rooted in money, what kind of decisions will that motivate you to make? What kind of person will you end up becoming? Remember that closing the gap between our actual, ought, and ideal selves is what drives our behavior. If your ideal self is rich, then you will continue to make decisions to get richer. You may even sacrifice important values (like honesty) in order to achieve it. We've all heard the Bible verse "money is the root of all evil." But the actual verse is "the *love* of money is the root of all evil." Money isn't evil in and of itself, but our endless desire to accumulate it leads some people to do some real shady shit.

That's not to say that you can't value your career. Assigning value to success at work (that probably comes with some money) doesn't necessarily create negative self-guides within you. I have friends who value career success above most other things who are still extremely happy, who still have wonderful, healthy relationships, and who don't spend their lives wishing they had more. Their desire to succeed drives them to be better, to do more, and growing toward that success fulfills them. I also derive internal esteem from a well-done project and external esteem when I hear praise from a client. There's absolutely nothing wrong with that.

I'm not here to tell you what you're supposed to value in life (unless it's money, in which case, don't). I'm here to point out the things that may be leading to your feelings of lack and unhappiness. Too many of us chase career success solely to gain external esteem—the feeling that you've "made it" when you finally get that big promotion and can upgrade from a Hyundai to a Lexus. But all too often and all too quickly it becomes about nothing other than money. Because money is the way we display that success to the world. Otherwise, how would they know? My Singaporean friend recently told me about the "Five Cs of Success" in Singapore: Cash, Car, Credit Card, Condo, Caucasian. That's right. Dating a white person is key to proving you've "made it" in Singapore.

And what if you're not traditionally successful despite trying your best to play the game? You made money and success your ideal, but you can't seem to achieve it? How are you supposed to fill the chasm between your lofty dreams and your sputtering career without a case of wine and a pint of ice cream? Welp, first off, have a glass of wine. Fuck it, I'll have one too. Because if you fail at this goal to accumulate wealth, or if you succeed but keep moving the goal posts to acquire more and more wealth each year, you will be unhappy. Forever. Yikes.

I know what some of you are thinking . . . *I don't care that much about money or being super rich, but how can I be happy without it? Being poor is hard and sad!*

Excellent question, and great point. Being truly poor in America while being constantly inundated with the ideals of a late-stage capitalist society is most certainly hard and sad. Being unable to afford food for your family is even harder and sadder. But if you just mean poor as in, I have food and I pay my rent, but I can't afford designer clothes or fancy restaurants or a Mercedes, then you're not poor. There are plenty of happy people in the world with far less money than you.

According to a 2015 Pew Research Center study,[18] "Poor" is considered living on under $2.00 per day, "Low Income" is $2.01–$10 per day, and "High Income" is over $50 per day. Just 7 percent of the world made it into the "High Income" category. Fifty dollars a day works out to just $1,500 per month or $18,000 per year, which sits comfortably above the poverty line for a single person in the United States.[19] Do you live on less than that?

I have made significantly less money in all the years since I worked in finance (except one), and I have been infinitely happier for each of those years. And even though I'm comparatively poor next to most people I know in the United States (and remain "the poor one" of my very successful group of friends), I'm still objectively richer than at least 93 percent of the world's

---

[18]. Rakesh Kochhar, "A Global Middle Class Is More Promise than Reality," Pew Research Center, July 8, 2015, https://www.pewresearch.org/global/2015/07/08/a-global-middle-class-is-more-promise-than-reality/.

[19]. $12,880 is the poverty line for a single person in 2021. I think we can all agree this number should be updated. "2021 Poverty Guidelines," Office of the Assistant Secretary for Planning and Evaluation, https://aspe.hhs.gov/topics/poverty-economic-mobility/poverty-guidelines/prior-hhs-poverty-guidelines-federal-register-references/2021-poverty-guidelines.

population, and probably closer to 98. Seventy-one percent of the world lives on less than $10 a day. Never forget that fun fact. Does living on less than $10 a day mean you will definitely be unhappy? Of course not!

If you were born in Cambodia, your whole ten-person family might live in a one-room house, and you all work the rice paddies, and you only own two shirts each. But so does everyone else you know. You are happy because you aren't going hungry, and your family is healthy, and you are blessed with the good fortune of not starving. If they had ten million dollars, would they be happier? You may think, *Of course they would be*, but you would be wrong.

This brings me to the inequality of comparison. If everyone around you is living in a one-room house with ten people, and that's the only life you know, it's impossible to want what you don't know you don't have. But the more proximity you have to the level of wealth you haven't attained, the starker that difference is. I have millionaire friends who live in some of the wealthiest neighborhoods in the country, but insist they are "middle class" because they only make mid-six-figures, and everyone around them makes five or ten times more. In fact, only 11 percent of the wealthiest 5 percent of Americans (those worth $5 million or more) describe themselves as "wealthy or rich."[20] The rest consider themselves "middle class" or "upper middle class." The problem with the "one percent" is that it includes both people who make $600,000 a year . . . and Jeff Bezos. Of course you're going to say you're not that rich when the guy down the street owns a private jet.

Living in Cape Town, South Africa, some of the poorest people in the *world* live just minutes from one of the wealthiest suburbs in the country. Most of Cape Town's townships (the informal settlements of corrugated metal shacks scattered

---

[20.] Robert Frank, "Most millionaires say they're middle class," CNBC, May 6, 2015, https://www.cnbc.com/2015/05/06/naires-say-theyre-middle-class.html.

around the city) are filled with people living on less than $1 a day.[21] Can you imagine living in Beverly Hills staring at sprawling multi-million-dollar mansions while scraping by on just $2 or $3 a day? Because that's the equivalent. And that kind of stark inequality is what leads to feelings of frustration and unhappiness, and in South Africa's case, crime.

Your feelings of not having enough are likely much more closely related to how much you're comparing yourself to those around you than any real affliction you're suffering. There are people in the one percent making $600,000 a year who are living beyond their means and feel like their budget is stretched thin, and there are people making $40,000 a year who are happily tucking away savings (it me).

As long as you are measuring your own success and self-worth in terms of the money you make, and the car you drive, and the square footage of your house, you will always be miserable. Because you can ALWAYS be richer, and you can always be more successful, until you're Bill Gates. But now Jeff Bezos is coming in hot and suddenly you're not the richest man in the world anymore! Oh shit, now it's Elon! There are people with millions upon millions—and even billions—of dollars who still wish they had more. Why? Because for every echelon of wealth you rise up into, there are other people doing even more exclusive rich people things for even richer people. It's never enough. As long as your own levels of happiness and satisfaction are tied to any external, materialistic factors, you're chasing a stuffed rabbit around a track.

I know millennials have had it bad in the U.S. I know we've already lived through two recessions, we still have insane amounts of student loans, there is yet another housing bubble pricing us out of ever owning a home, and any generational wealth transfer (if you're privileged enough to be expecting

---

[21.] Robert Gastaldo, "Cape Flat Townships," Colby Community College Web, accessed February 17, 2022, http://web.colby.edu/ragastal/travels/south-africa/cape-flat-townships/.

this) is gonna have to wait another thirty years since modern medicine has our wonderful Boomer parents living to 100 (sorry Mom, I love you). I know the minimum wage is far from livable (even that $15 we haven't achieved already isn't nearly enough), and there are very real inequality and cost-of-living problems in the United States. And what's this about stagflation? Dear lord, when will it end? That being said, whatever amount of money you think you need to live, I promise you it's a lot less. And if you can really distill your life to just the things the matter—if you don't buy new clothes every month, and you drive a used car you bought with cash, and you live in a perfectly cozy yet slightly shittier apartment a little further from town—you'll realize you have a lot more money than you thought you did.[22]

Before we go on, I want to be abundantly clear here: money does buy *some* happiness. Having unlimited money means unlimited freedom, and you never have to work for some boss you hate or clean toilets or worry about getting sick in our dystopian nightmare of a healthcare system. If you have a business idea, you can just start it; if you want to go somewhere, you book a ticket. Ya' don't need running shoes to go running, but they sure fockin' help.

I'm not idealizing being poor or suggesting it's better than having a million bucks in your bank account. I'm just trying to help you understand that you don't need as much as you think you do. And at the end of the day, all the clothes and cars and fancy apartments don't make us any happier. In fact, we are likely no happier as a society than our hunter-gatherer ancestors. Other than the invention of eyeglasses and the discovery of antibiotics, I'm pretty sure they were better off than we are.

[22.] I'll add this caveat one last time as a member of the subreddit /r/povertyfinance: I know this isn't true for everyone, and I know there aren't magical bootstraps to pull yourself up by. But it is true for some people, and this is directed toward them. If you're already living on the bare minimum, trust me, I've been there. Keep working, keep fighting for change. Vote for people who want to raise the minimum wage and tie it to inflation. Join a union. Try to slowly move your way up in higher-paying jobs to get your head above water. It sucks, but you can do it.

They worked fewer hours to meet their needs, had closer familial and societal bonds, and didn't spend two hundred dollars a week to see a therapist for their depression caused by being such a miserable failure.

As anthropologist and author James Suzman discusses in his book *Affluence without Abundance*, the concept of happiness in the bushman tribes of Southern Africa is based on fulfilling limited needs that are immediately met. There is no concept of *I'm going to be happy once I have this.* There is no such thing as "future happiness." Happiness is only a thing you are or are not feeling right now, like anger, or pain when you stub your toe. And when your immediate needs are met, then you want for nothing. And without the gap between what you want and what you have, there is nothing making you feel inadequate.

To understand why our desire for things is what's making us unhappy, we can look to the desire-fulfillment theory[23] of well-being. The root of desire-fulfillment theory is simple: you will be happy if you achieve or acquire what you desire, and unhappy if you don't. I'm not sure I'm fully on board with using desire to define happiness, but I agree with the underlying supposition here: the less you desire, the more likely you are to be happy. If you live a life where you are constantly wanting for something *more*, you will always be unhappy. If you desire only what you already have, you will have nothing left to desire, and you will already be happy. The concept aligns with self-discrepancy: unhappiness is rooted in the difference between our expectations and reality.

You want money so badly because you have been fed the idea that if you can just get these things, you will be happy. You want designer clothes so badly because you're convinced you will be sexier, more confident, people will envy you, people will want to be you, and you'll get that esteem we're all so desperately craving. You are constantly faced with people around you

---

[23]. Derek Parfit, "What Makes Someone's Life Go Best," *Reasons and Persons*, (1984), https://rintintin.colorado.edu/~vancecd/phil1100/Parfit1.pdf.

who have more, who look better, who embody the things you desire. You are forced into comparative poverty every time you can't afford something that someone else has. Your mid-size sedan and your shitty apartment remind you daily that you do not have a Mercedes and a penthouse. Your Mercedes and your penthouse remind you that you don't have a Lamborghini and a private island. Happiness in modern society has become a monetary end-game—it is a goal to be achieved by bridging the gap between wants and haves, but there is always infinitely more to want.

With the recent growth of the minimalist movement and the tiny house movement, it's clear that more and more people are understanding this fundamental truth: that we have too many things and that those things never provide the happiness and fulfillment they promise. We buy bigger homes to fill them with even more stuff; we spend more money than we have, we go into debt, and for whom? For ourselves? Has anything you bought ever made you truly happy?

Sure, when you first got your new iPhone, you were so excited. But I'm sure that slowly morphed into complaining about it. Your new car you loved isn't so shiny and new anymore, but it's still costing you $600 a month. No one is immune. Of course I feel happy and excited when I buy a new sweater that I love (I really love sweaters) or when we got our Nintendo Switch during lockdown (I told you, I like nice things too). But *things* will never be a real or lasting source of happiness. Deep down, I know you know that. But the temporary high you get from them is enough to keep you going until it comes time to fill the void with something else.

If the entire world was Cambodian rice paddies and you were the only one with a Hyundai Sonata and three bedrooms in your house, do you think you would you be happier? Would you be happier knowing you had more than everyone else, that you possessed everything there was to own? I would argue you would probably feel worse, and also ostracized from everyone else. Or what if you knew about penthouses and Bentleys and diamonds,[24] but no one else did ... would you still want them? If you are surrounded by people who are completely happy with so much less than you have, it is impossible not to realize how meaningless the pursuit of material wealth is as an end in itself. I dare you to try it.

A few studies have come out in the last ten years attempting to prove once and for all that money doesn't buy happiness. The first was a study by two Nobel laureates and Princeton professors, Daniel Kahneman and Angus Deaton, back in 2010,[25] and the next was a 2016 study by economist David Clingingsmith at Case Western Reserve University.[26] Their findings both agreed that money does increase happiness, but only up to a certain point. Kahneman and Deaton said that point was $75,000 (about $100,000 today) and Clingingsmith found that point to be $80,000 of household income with diminishing returns up to $200,000 (about $106,000 and $265,000 in today's dollars, respectively). Basically saying, you still get happier after $100,000 but not as much as getting to that point. That tipping point is the amount it takes for you to be comfortable and do what you want and not have to worry about money. Makes sense. If money is a daily stress, and you're never one hundred percent sure if you can pay your bills each month, having more money can make you happier—like, so much happier and also physically healthier. Living in poverty literally kills you. But if your basic needs are already met, and you can treat yourself to dinners out every so often and a couple vacations a year, more money isn't gonna do the trick. That's the idea.

[24.] Don't even get me started on the worthlessness of diamonds.

[25.] Daniel Kahneman and Angus Deaton, "High income improves evaluation of life but not emotional well-being," Proceedings of the National Academy of Sciences of the United States of America, (September 2010), https://www.pnas.org/content/107/38/16489.

[26.] David Clingingsmith, "Negative Emotions, Income, and Welfare," Department of Economics, Case Western Reserve University, (September 2015), https://www.academia.edu/11407739/Negative_Emotions_Income_and_Welfare

But interestingly enough, a 2021 study from the Wharton School[27] found that there was no such bar at $80,000 or $90,000, but that people just keep on getting happier the richer they get. Well, fuck me. I guess you can just put this book down right now and get back on that hamster wheel to financial success! Just kidding. There is a caveat here that was conveniently left out of most the headlines talking about this study: that happiness was directly correlated to whether or not the subjects thought money was important:

> Low earners were happier if they thought money was unimportant and high earners were happier if they thought money was important . . . However, the more people equated money and success, the lower their experienced well-being was on average, and there did not appear to be any income level at which equating money and success was associated with greater experienced well-being.

"The more people equated money and success, the lower their experienced well-being was on average." If you think money is important and defines your success, you will be unhappy without it. But if you don't, you don't need it. You get to decide what is and is not important in your life and what defines your own happiness. How fucking incredible is that?

When my soul-searching, life-affirming solo year abroad came to an unwilling end, I returned to the U.S. with the sole purpose of saving up money to travel again. I had learned how

---

[27.] Matthew Killingsworth, "Experienced well-being rises with income, even above $75,000 per year," Proceedings of the National Academy of Sciences of the United States of America, (January 2021), https://www.pnas.org/content/118/4/e2016976118.

to live on nothing. I had learned how to see a quarter gleaming on the sidewalk. I had learned the value of a dollar for the first time in my life. I had found my purpose; all I needed was the money to do it. So I got a job waiting tables. One year later, and I was right back in Charlotte.

One afternoon, at one of those tables, one of my old finance colleagues came in for a business lunch. When he saw me come up to his table, his head cocked sympathetically to the side (why are people always doing that to me?) and he said, "Oh, you're working *here* now? How *are* things?" His voice and expression were drenched in pity—he saw I had clearly hit rock bottom, and this was the best I could do. He knew I was poor and just scraping by, but I wanted to shout in his face how wrong he was.[28] Well, he wasn't wrong, I was objectively poor even by American standards. But what he didn't realize was that I was a million times happier working my shift for almost no money, saving my pennies to travel, than I ever was in that office. And that is something he would probably never be able to understand. It is possible to be happier with less. It is possible to only want as much as money as you actually need.

I knew I wanted to travel, I knew I wanted to write, and I knew that working in a bar was the way to get that done. I knew that moving in with a friend, and never going out, and putting every penny I could into my piggy bank would make me happy. Because it was allowing me to do the one thing I knew I wanted to do. Because these actions were in line with my authentic ideal. Even if it would take me six months or eight months or two years to save up the money I needed. I was working toward my ideal self, my ideal life, every day.

My colleague could have offered me my cushy job and my cushy salary and my cushy finance bonuses right there on the spot, and I would have told him to go fuck himself. Just kidding, Bryan was one of the good ones. But there is nothing

---

[28.] I recently spoke with Bryan about this interaction, which he obviously does not recall. His answer? "If anything, I was jealous."

that could have convinced me to take it back. By all accounts, I was a failure. All of society probably saw me as a failure. My own mother surely thought I was a failure. I doubt I was even making minimum wage at that bar. And yet somehow, I was happy.

a tree-cloud interlude

the anatomy of regret

Now that you've come this far, I hope you're feeling uncomfortable. I hope that you were able to find some answers about how you got to where you are in your life. I hope you've found the things that you want to change if you weren't already aware of what those were. I hope you're ready to change them now that you do. I hope if you've always wanted to move to Paris that you are planning to move to fucking Paris.

But maybe as you've been looking at all the things you want to change, you've come across a few that you can't. That one thing (or the million things) you wished you had done differently, the branches you didn't follow, the ones you tried to follow but broke as soon as you took the first step. You know what I'm talking about: regret.

Regret can be a whisper, or it can be an ache. Regret can slowly eat away at the life you're living until you're left doubting everything it touches. The word regret feels like running in place. It is us running from ourselves, but there's nowhere to go. Regret can keep quiet for days or months, but it never disappears. We never forget the things we regret. It is a single word that signifies our own unhappiness. It spreads through our thoughts like a virus, vile and viscous and poisonous. It is a word that reminds us that we have done something wrong, that there are things we wish to change, but can't. It haunts us without end.

Maybe it was bullying that girl in middle school or letting a drunk friend drive your car. Maybe it was turning down a great job offer to stay with a shitty guy. Bummer. Regret lives in the biggest branches of our tree-clouds and the most infinitesimal minutiae: the decisions that didn't affect anything at all but still linger with you years later. That time you embarrassed yourself in front of the whole party. That one girl you slept with when you shouldn't have.

Not all regrets, however, are equal. Some change the course of your life in an immutable way. Some don't matter at all. And some possibly changed the course of someone else's life. But there is one thing that all regrets have in common: we can't change them. We can't change what we did or said, ever. We can't take back our actions, no matter how ashamed of them we are. We can't choose a different branch of the tree-cloud any more than we can un-cheat on our boyfriends or un-plagiarize that essay. You can't make your brain forget it, and you can't erase it.

But if we understand why we regret a certain decision, maybe we can understand enough about ourselves to regret fewer decisions. Maybe regret can be the thing that makes us better—maybe it's one of the things that makes us who we are.

I'm sure this has brought up something that you regret, whether big or small. Now think about the why. Do you regret something you did or said because it cost you a job or a relationship? Because it was immoral or unethical? Do you regret the action or just the consequences of it? Do you regret something because it made you seem stupid or uncool? Do you regret doing something that was honestly terrible because you hurt another person and you wish you hadn't? I'm sorry, Stephanie.

If you regret the consequences of an action but not the action itself (i.e., I regret cheating on my wife because I got caught, not I regret cheating on my wife because I love her, and that's not the kind of partner I want to be) then you are doomed to repeat your mistakes. Good luck. I cannot help you. But if you truly regret the action itself, it's because you saw a version of yourself you don't want to be. Maybe you were filling a void with a temporary pleasure, and you know that's not who you really are. Or maybe you were working toward a version of your ought or ideal self, and that regret is telling you you've been working toward the wrong thing.

Think how that regret might have changed you. Was it a paradigm-shifting moment? Think about the person you became after that regret. Did you lose some money on a risky investment and then became overly cautious as a result? Did you lose the woman you loved because you were a dick, and now you're definitely never gonna be that guy again? Maybe for you, you went to art school instead of business school and that was the wrong branch in your life. Maybe you hate yourself for wasting so much time. Maybe your ideal self values financial security and taking care of your family more than following your passion, and that's okay too. Because it means you learned something about who you want to be—about what matters most to you—in the process.

Whether tree branch or tiny twig, once you understand how that regrettable action fits into your path and what you would have done differently, that regret becomes a part of the next iteration of you. The you who changes every day. The you who is never set in stone. That lesson learned, that ideal discovered, whatever it is would not exist without the mistake. Every one of those embarrassing moments, every mortifying, regrettable choice is indivisible from your very identity and plays a part in every decision you make going forward, whether you're self-aware enough to see it or not.

Coming to terms with these terrible choices we've made, whether life-altering or barely on the radar, isn't always easy, but it's doable. We know exactly why we regret a thing we did—because we saw the outcome it had in our lives. *If only I hadn't* . . . . But as you've been simmering in your own choices and pondering the worst ones you've ever made (fun, right?), it's probably the other kind of regret, the more insidious kind, that you just can't seem to let go of: *If only I had* . . .

No one is immune from imagining the possibilities of alternative lives, of regretting the paths they didn't take. Even if you aren't haunted by it, even if it doesn't feel like a mistake no one is exempt from thinking one different decision could have changed their trajectory, could have made things better, could have fixed whatever is wrong with the life they are living. I think we may all be a little obsessed with the idea that one of these alternate lives would have been the perfect one.

If only I had taken that job . . . if only I had told her I loved her . . . if only I had gone to business school instead of art school.

Of course, there is no way to know what that life would have been like, and we are programmed to idealize situations in which we can never be proven wrong. That life is better than this one because I'm not living in that one. The grass is always greener. But regretting a branch of the tree-cloud you didn't follow is like trying to catch a falling knife with a blindfold on. You'll never see where it would have landed, and if you do catch it, it'll make your hands bleed. There's no way to rewind; there's no choice to unchoose. It's only forward we go.

But how can you let it go when that other life is so perfect . . . the one where you get the job and the girl and everything you've always wanted?

The best way (the only way) to deal with the decisions that erased a version of you who existed on another branch is to see every choice you've made as an integral part of the person you've become. It's to realize that the person in that other life isn't even you.

Would I be the same person I am without getting addicted to cocaine or quitting the engineering program? Without getting made fun of in middle school or being fake in high school or getting my heart broken or having a career I never wanted? Without falling in love with a poet who ghosted me only to have my fuck buddy from college tell me I should move to New Zealand? Each of those events in this version of my life, each of my embarrassing mistakes and every skeleton in my closet is an inextricable part of who I am today—even the ones that still hurt to remember. Who would I even be without those things? I learned a job I didn't want, and a boy I didn't want, and learned how to pick up the pieces when everything goes to shit, how to come out stronger on the other side.

Had you taken another path with different mistakes, maybe you wouldn't even want the things you want now. Had you married the girl instead of taking that job in London, maybe you would have spent your whole life dreaming of the big city. You didn't know you cared more about this thing until you made the choice that took it away. And if you made the other choice, you might never have even learned that about yourself. We stupid humans only ever seem to learn lessons the hard way.

And even if that other choice was the right one, even if you truly never should have taken that job and let the love of your life slip away, I promise you'd still be wanting and wishing for other things you couldn't have. Had you been more successful in this imaginary life, maybe you wouldn't have been as kind. Maybe you would have cheated on your husband or gotten so depressed from your high-pressure job that you started contemplating suicide. Who knows why human nature is for us to be eternally unsatisfied, but that's the lot we got.

The only way to escape the *shoulda coulda wouldas* in your life is to start making more choices in line with your authentic ideal self. And the more closely aligned with your authentic ideal self you become, the less you're going to regret. Seriously, they studied it. According to a 2018 study published in the journal *Emotion*,[29] it's the regrets of *in*action related to our unrealized ideal selves that cause the most long-term sorrow, the most enduring regrets. We spend our lives making choices to please our ought selves, then spend the rest of our lives wishing we'd done the thing that our ideal selves wanted instead. And the most painful of those regrets are almost always the things we didn't do, not the ones we tried and failed at.

Obviously, this tracks. Everyone knows that whenever

[29.] Shai Davidai and Thomas Gilovh, (2018). "The ideal road not taken: The self-discrepancies involved in people's most enduring regrets." *Emotion*, 18(3), 439–452. https://doi.org/10.1037/emo0000326.

anyone asks a bunch of old people what they regret, it's the things they didn't do. And it pretty much never has anything to do with money. Not spending enough time with your family, not traveling the world when you had the chance, not telling that one friend that you love her. Those regrets stay with us because you can never know what it would have been. There is no consequence to understand or to synthesize into who you are—it's only questions about a better version of your life. Your unrealized ideal.

But when you finally embrace the thing you know you should have done so long ago, there is no regret on the other side. When you finally leave your shitty group of friends who do nothing but make you feel bad about yourself. When you finally tell your boss that you're quitting to write a book or travel the world or both. When you finally have the courage to tell a joke to a group of people. Even if you fail. Even if your book sucks. Even if you come back home from Paris after three weeks because it turns out you hate the fucking French.[30] When you start making choices in line with your authentic ideal self—even if they seem crazy or scary or stupid—you won't regret them. You won't regret those things because you finally listened to yourself for once. You climbed out on that branch of your tree-cloud and maybe realized, okay, this wasn't it. But you learned something new about yourself and another new branch was created.

No branch of the tree-cloud, whether in the past or starting today, is a recipe for perfection, because—and I hate to be the one to break this to you—there is no perfect life. Even if you start making choices aligned with your authentic ideal self right now this very moment, you're still going to make mistakes. And those mistakes are going to be a part of the person you are and the person you want to be just as much as all those other stupid things you did.

---

[30]. This is a terrible American stereotype—French people are wonderful.

We all have moments we want to undo, moments we should have been a better version of ourselves. And that's okay. It's okay to make mistakes because everyone does. All the time. As long as you learn from them. As long as you let those shitty branches remind you of the person you need to be. That's part of the miraculous beauty of our tree-clouds. We don't have to live in the past or regret the past because we are making new futures for ourselves every day.

september 2009

    Suddenly I am faced with the biggest decision of my life—with the choice to stay and be responsible or to run away from everything—my debt, my job, my apartment, my life. I envision the next decade and all the things I won't do. I will not buy a house. I will not buy a car. I will not move into a fancy apartment building or get any job that requires a credit check. But I don't care. And it liberates me. That flip book isn't my life, it is someone else's, and the more I think about all of the things I am supposed to want, the less I want them. Suddenly the three-thousand-dollar bag on my arm and the seven-hundred-dollar shoes on my feet that I once coveted and adored metamorphose into the dull, greyed steel of the bars on my cell, of the chains on my feet. I am going mad with a desire for freedom. Nothing can possibly stop the inevitable string of events that one sunset somehow set into motion.

    This massive decision that has only frustrated and petrified me in the past suddenly makes me dizzy with excitement. I could be free. But what will I do? I don't want a mortgage or a car payment. I don't want to sit behind another corporate desk for the rest of my life, and every molecule in my being knows this. As with every action and reaction in life, there are reactants, catalysts, and conditions required to yield the final product. After four years in a city I ended up living in by an inexplicably fucked up string of unpredictable events, I now find myself leaving in the same fashion. The dominoes of the universe that will inevitably tumble, I cannot, or will not fight. It no longer feels like a choice, but a fate to which I have submitted. And with each day that passes I search only for the excuse, for the final catalyst, for the way out.

    I am scared. Or, maybe, I should be. I am not. All I know is that everything I thought was right for the last four years has been wrong. Perhaps the dreamed stereotype of a well-manicured lawn, and a nice car, and a few properly educated kids will bring happiness to most. Perhaps my ravenous thirst for freedom is an anomaly in a sea of people who fit a bill I was never meant to pay. Regardless, as it is yet again, I don't know what I want, but I know without a doubt what I don't. It is crazy, I am crazy, so they tell me. But not a second of these years has been wasted if it took every one of them to cement in me the knowledge that none of this is anything I want for myself. Everyone I know, most of my friends, especially my family, think this is the most wildly irresponsible decision I have made in an absurdly long string of wildly irresponsible decisions. Despite this, and surprisingly, most of them understand. This life is not for me.

The moment the decision is made, despite every wild, unwoven thread of my poorly sewn plan, I know there isn't any other way. I don't have time to bide reason or responsibility. Responsibility will cost me a decade. There are many choices in life you can't unchoose, but few of which are given the grace of a second thought, the respect of a shred of a regret. This is the all the former, and none of the latter.

I am finally free.

on running away

I think it's time to address the elephant in this book. I told you I ran away and moved to New Zealand and changed my whole perspective on shit, but you have probably been wondering this whole time, *How the fuck did this chick just run away to New Zealand? I'd like to run away to New Zealand! What about all that credit card debt she keeps talking about?*

I knew I needed to leave Charlotte. I knew I needed to quit my job. But even if you have figured out exactly what you want, it doesn't always make it easy to do. I can say it's easy to quit your job and join the circus, but you still have to get into trapeze school first. So I made a plan. And then another plan. And then none of the plans I made ended up being the correct plan. As it turns out, none of the plans I made ever included moving to New Zealand in the first place. But I thought it was only fair to show you my road map rather than acting like one of those articles headlined, "How This Enterprising Millennial Became a Millionaire by 30" and then you find out it's because their parents were already millionaires who paid the down payment on their house and also hired them as CEO at the tech company they owned. I'm aware my story has plenty of white privilege, just not that much.

When I got back from the Serengeti, I signed up for creative writing classes at UNCC after work to help build my portfolio so I could apply to MFA programs that winter. I would have sixty thousand more dollars of debt to move into a decidedly unlucrative career (if I even got accepted), but it was the only way I could envision escaping and aligning my life with the ideal self I had discovered.

Then, yet again, in the strange way that my entire life seems to be based on one-off comments from other people that they definitely don't remember saying, these socially acceptable, semi-responsible plans were upended by a passing thought or possibly even a joke from my brother-in-law, nudging that first domino to fall:

You know, you should probably just run away from all of your debt.

Now, I know this sounds like terrible advice. To put this into perspective, my brother-in-law is also in finance and is traditionally successful (read: rich AF). He didn't just utter these words and walk away. He explained exactly why, at twenty-five, I was better off to leave all the debt, travel the world, and come back in three years debt-free[31] (save for my student loans, of course, which follow you to your grave) than I was to sit there for years paying it off. And he wasn't wrong. At the rate I was going, in ten years, I still wouldn't have come close to paying all that off.

To be clear, I am not recommending everyone who is struggling to keep up with minimum payments suddenly runs away from it all. It was an irresponsible choice at best, and it was even more irresponsible for me to run up that debt in the first place. There are massive downsides and repercussions to this decision, and I did not take it lightly. My roommate at the time agreed in advance to handle the flood of mail that was sure to come for me as creditors hunted me down. Creditors started hounding my mother before long. She started telling them she had never heard of me. I hadn't even met my husband when this happened,

---

[31]. Three years is the statute of limitations on debt collection in North Carolina. It varies state by state. After this time, they can't sue you or garnish your wages, but they can sure as shit keep harassing you about it. Seven years is a good general measure to be free and clear.

but years later as the debts were sold and resold for pennies on the dollar, they started calling my mother-in-law.

I knew that I was not going to be able to rent an apartment that required a credit check or get a cell phone contract when I came back. I knew that I would likely never have a credit card, and I wouldn't be buying a house for a very long time. But I didn't want those things. I didn't want any debt ever again the rest of my life. Debt was a prison that I had created. Debt was the bars on the cell keeping me in Charlotte. Fuck debt. Fuck finance. Fuck it all.

If you are drowning in debt, you can also go the more conventional way and declare bankruptcy, but honestly, thirteen years later, I have perfect credit, no bankruptcy on my record, and my brother-in-law was 100 percent right. I wouldn't say I'm proud of the choice that I made (or so many of the choices that led to that choice), but I don't regret any of them for a second. It was what I needed to do for me; it was my only way out. And since I'm here to tell you to do what you want and not how to do what I think you should do, then please go ahead and do whatever the fuck you want.

And so, one September afternoon, with eight thousand dollars of availability on a line of credit (that I only had because I had drunk driven my car into a ditch and the insurance paid out more than the car was worth)[32] I walked into the bank sweating like I might rob the place. In a way, I was. I requested to draw down the entire line in cash. As the nice teller lady dropped the pile of money into the whizzing money-counting machine, I looked around nervously as if the police were suddenly going to swarm around me, as if they knew that I was never coming back. No one said a word. The cashier handed me an envelope thick with possibility, and I walked back out to my car, my hands shaking with nerves and excitement and fear. With that, I said goodbye to the only future I had ever known. I quit my job

---

[32.] I know, I know, so many things I'm not proud of, but #treecloud.

with an unceremonious exit interview questionnaire reading: "Reason for Leaving: Fuck Finance."

Of course, if we know anything about our own tree-clouds by now, life often decides that the plans we make are not at all what is going to happen.

when things fall apart

With eight thousand dollars cash in my suitcase, I flee to DC in the adrenaline rush of an indelible decision. I burn every bridge with the world of finance, with my last employer, with my former self. Even if I want to, I can never go back. But I already know that will never happen. I close all my bank accounts. I keep the cash in a hole I cut in my pillow. I change my phone number. I have no address. I am off the grid. I am finally free.

I have a place to stay in DC for a few months, living in the sunroom of one of my closest friends, cleaning her house in exchange for cheaper rent. I know I need to find an income before I tear through the cash I have in the same manner I have torn through every other amount of money that has ever touched my hands. The financial analyst who can't manage her own finances amuses me even in destitution. Within a couple weeks I have my very first waitressing job. This is the life I want. I will write during the day while everyone is at work. I will wait tables into the early hours of morning to pay my bills. I will survive this way, and I will answer to no one. I will do what I love without compromising myself. I am finally living for me.

But my ideal life is nothing but a mirage wavering ever further in the distance. Getting off at three a.m. I end up drinking until sunrise and sleeping until my shift begins again at five. I am not writing. There is nothing creative coming from me except the words for the poet I believe myself to love—he, a piece of this great catalyst in the first place, this barreling freight train towards freedom. But the words that he ignited within me now fall limp on unrequited ears. I guess he only loved me from 400 miles away.

Where is my great creative spark? This great drive that will blossom into a book? As the snow stands in dirtied mountain ranges across the city, I spend my time with friends and bourbon. I am drunk every day yet again. *It's alright for now*, I tell myself. *I have only just quit. I can take this time to have a little fun. Everything will fall into place as it should. I am just getting acclimated to this new life.*

Three weeks into my very first waitressing gig, I am fired for having a beer on the clock. I cry when they call and tell me never to come in again. It is mid-December, and I have no idea what I am going to do. In a drunken night desperate for what little attention the poet would so flippantly dangle in front of me, I let his intoxicated friend drive my Jeep. He drives it into a light post and disappears. I have torn through more than two thousand dollars in just a few weeks and now have no income. But a week before Christmas is no time to look for a job. I wipe the tears from my eyes and resign myself to enjoy Christmas and my birthday and look for a new job after the new year. I turn twenty-six on New Year's Day, and I believe wholly that this new year will be new in every way for me. At twenty-six I will finally know what I should have learned about myself at twenty. I trust in the universe to tell me what to do. I believe this when I say it. I am utterly lost.

how did i get here?

We've talked about listening to the little voice. We've talked about following our paths through to the people we are now and the people we want to become . . . but what do you do when every choice you're making is the wrong one? What do you do when every plan you had turns to shit, when you have no idea what the fuck you're supposed to do next? What do you do when life just fucking sucks?

If all of your decisions in life thus far have been the right ones, and circumstance has never given your tree-cloud a good shake, then congratulations. I'd like you to go buy a plane ticket to Aruba and enjoy being oblivious to adversity; it comes with its own set of problems. For the rest of us, there will be things that went wrong, things that pushed us to places we weren't planning on going. There will be chains of events started by a thing we never saw coming. There will be ways we react we couldn't have predicted, and moments that ended up defining us out of nowhere—for better or for worse. Some people overcome adversity; others get swallowed by it. Sometimes a branch of the tree-cloud lands on your fucking car, and you gotta start taking the bus to work.

When the things that happen in our lives are based on our own choices, we can feel regret, we can wish we'd followed the other branch, but when we're in shitty situations due to circumstances completely beyond our control, it's tempting to shake our fists at the sky and proclaim that life just isn't fair. Well, you're not wrong. Life most certainly isn't fair. Some people have it easy, and some people most certainly don't. Some people can make all the right choices and still end up with the worst fucking luck.

Maybe that's how you're feeling at this very moment. Maybe your life didn't turn out the way you thought it would, but when you look back at the branches that led you to where you are, it's just not your fault. *My mom got sick, and I got so behind on bills. There weren't any good jobs after college, so I got stuck in this dead-end company. I grew up in a shitty home without any support, so it's always been hard for me. I couldn't afford to move to the city, so I had to move back home. My girlfriend is a bitch who cheated on me, so now I am depressed and alone.* It's just the way things are, and life is always gonna be shitty because that's the lot you got. It was just the hand you were dealt.

Whether bad luck and tragedy have defined your life or are just a passing stage, we've all had these thoughts at one point or another. And they all share one distinct thread: they are each framed as a lack of control—as a lack of choice. Your life is something that happened to you. Some greater external force pushed you into this situation. It's not your fault. Again, you're not wrong. And all of these are real, valid reasons to be pissed off. Sometimes life just screws you over, and there is absolutely nothing you can do about it.

But I'm here to remind you that even in the midst of circumstances completely beyond your control, you still have a choice. You always have a choice.[33] We don't just choose what we do, we choose every single day how we react to the things that happen to us. Whether the fucked-up branch of your tree-cloud is a choice you made that went awry or just another way the world screwed you over—it's always still up to you to choose. You get to choose what you do next. You get to choose who you want to be. You get to choose how happy you are every single day.

Some people are born billionaires and others are born into

---

[33]. I'd like to note here that the ability to change your circumstances is most certainly a privilege in itself. Not everyone has the means, and the choices they do have are extremely limited. That being said, there are still options. Send me an email and I'll help you figure it out. Seriously.

poverty in a wildly racist and unjust society. Some people have to work much harder to achieve the same level of personal and financial success. Some people have to fight through childhood traumas just to fucking exist in this world. You didn't choose to grow up in a shitty town, and you didn't choose for your parents to fight every single night. Those are things that just happened to you. But you did choose how you reacted to them. And how you continue to react to them each and every day.

You may be miserable because your girlfriend left you, but why did that happen? And what are you gonna do about it? Maybe your job sucks, but does that mean the rest of your life has to suck? It is so incredibly easy to absolve ourselves of responsibility when things don't go our way. It's tempting to be unhappy because it means you don't have to do anything about it. But what good does it do us? All it does is cement our own dissatisfaction. How can you be happy when you work at McDonald's and you don't a have a girlfriend? How can you be happy when everything is always going wrong?? No amount of "finding authenticity" is going to fix your shitty job and your shitty situation. We surrender our own happiness because we just can't win against the forces of fate.

Welp, I hate to break it to you, but while circumstance has a lot to do with where you end up financially—like when your rich parents bought you that house and made you CEO at age twenty-four[34]—it has very little effect on how happy you are. A 2008 study conducted by researchers at the University of Illinois[35] found that the average happiness rating of people who think happiness is controllable is 7.39 (out of 10). For the people who believe happiness is out of their control, the average drops down to 5.61.

---

[34]. Sorry, very successful white dude who was born into a wealthy family, you didn't just work harder than everyone else to get where you are.

[35]. Pelin Kesebir and Ed Diener, "In Pursuit of Happiness: Empirical Answers to Philosophical Questions," *Perspectives on Psychological Science*, 3, (March 2008): 117–25, https://doi.org/10.1111/j.1745-6916.2008.00069.x.

I don't care where you are in your life or how bad things are. For most of us, at some point, circumstance will give our tree-clouds a pretty good shake and screw up everything we thought we were going to do. You can let that ruin you, or you can not. At the end of the day, life will always be okay as long as you're okay with whatever life is. You will be happy as long as you choose to be happy. Blaming other people for your circumstances—even when they are 100 percent not your fault, and even if they are definitely 100 percent Linda's fault—will only serve to make you more miserable. How can it possibly be anyone else's fault that you're miserable? Who is in control of your emotions other than yourself? Ask yourself *why* you feel miserable. Who are you blaming it on?

Maybe you were abused as a child; maybe your family was so poor that you were hungry all the time, and you never had clothes to wear to school. Maybe your parents were drunks, or they abandoned you at a gas station, and you were raised in an orphanage. For most of us, it probably wasn't all that bad, but we still had and have our own shit. Everyone's shit is valid because it is the only shit they've ever known. And for all those things you say, *This is why I am the way I am now. I can't change it; these things happened to me.*

While those things did happen to you, you are the way you are now because of how you have chosen to respond to those things every day since they happened. Every day one of those 35,000 choices was to continue letting that thing define you. Even if you've felt like a victim your entire life, you can choose to stop playing that part immediately. Right now. Today. Even if you truly have been a victim, it doesn't have to define you. You are always in control of your life. Here is how you do it. You say, *Okay, so some messed up shit happened to me, but what am I gonna do about it? Can I change any of it?* No. *Can I change the way I think about it?* Yes. And then you change it. You choose to be happy.

I know not everyone can afford therapy, and there are some people who honestly, truly need it to overcome the traumas they've endured. I'm not diminishing the damaging effects that trauma can have for even a heartbeat. I know clinical depression is real, and if you suffer from it, people telling you to "just be happy" can fuck right off. But I also believe there are a lot of us who just need help recognizing the self-talk that keeps us in negative patterns. The self-talk that lets you forgive yourself for not doing anything with your life because you had a hard childhood. It lets you absolve yourself of having healthy relationships because your parents were so dysfunctional. And while it may sound harder to take responsibility for everything that's happening in your life, the wonderful part is that it isn't—it makes everything better.

When you stop feeling like life just happened to you and you are a helpless victim of circumstance, it means you get to take control. It means you get to write your own narrative. It means your happiness goes from a 5 to a 7 because it's YOUR fucking life, and you're in control of it. It means you get to say fuck it and leave your shitty job or your shitty marriage or your shitty suburb and own your happiness every day. How fucking incredible is that?

No one is handed happiness in life. Kids born billionaires aren't born happy, and kids in the Cambodian rice paddies aren't born sad. We find it. We make it. We are either satisfied with our lives or dissatisfied with them, and that choice exists outside of wealth or circumstance or status or success. We all get dealt hands in life, some better than others, and we all have to choose how to respond to those hands.

When I was growing up, we moved every two years starting when I was six years old. And that was so hard on me. My childhood was difficult, and I was an angry, confused kid. With everything that was going on at school, I had no emotional regulation at home. I would fly off the handle at the slightest provocation. I would go to my room shaking, holding my knees trying to calm myself down while my sister whispered "pssyyyychooooo" into my ear. Siblings are cruel. My parents hated each other, and we would have these epic family fights nearly every week that all the neighborhood could hear, screaming and cursing and hurling insults across the room—all six of us. I didn't realize that this wasn't normal behavior until my mid-fucking-twenties. Seriously. I thought every family yelled like that; I didn't know anything else. My dad cheated on my mom endlessly; my mother played the martyr and stayed in a loveless marriage wallowing in self-pity rather than doing anything about it. I told my mom to divorce my dad when I was thirteen. She didn't listen until I was twenty-one. My dad's definition of being a good father was that he didn't beat us and we were never hungry, so by that measure, he was a great success. I didn't have the most traumatic childhood out there by a long shot, but the point is that we all have our shit.

All of these things could be reasons why I am a failure. I never adjusted socially after moving around so much. My parents' loveless marriage set a bad example for relationships, so now I only date shitty guys who cheat on me. I only ever knew how to scream and cry and throw things when I was angry, so that is still the way I am now. It doesn't matter if your childhood was traumatic or average or blissful, you can always find someone else to blame for your problems if you're looking.

Instead of looking at my childhood as a thing I had to overcome, I look at it as an integral part in shaping who I've become. Moving around so much forced me to become more outgoing and confident. Being fake all those years, trying to impress people and make friends, taught me how to be real and how to see authenticity in others. Seeing a damaged relationship showed me how to be healthy. For every event, every situation, you can see it from either of these sides. You can allow yourself to be a victim of your life, or you can empower yourself to learn and grow from the things that have happened to you.

Look at those things that happened in your life, those branches of your tree-cloud beyond your control. Follow a path to see them as part of making you a better person. Find a perspective that allows you to rewrite that narrative. No matter what happened to you, I promise it's possible. Because everyone has something bad that has happened to them. Some people have way more than others, for sure. But everyone has something.

Maybe you still feel like your life definitely would have been better if your parents hadn't been emotionally (or physically) abusive or you weren't bullied or you hadn't broken both of your legs, and maybe you're right. Or maybe breaking both your legs or getting diagnosed with cancer pushed you to a resilience that you never had before. Teddy Roosevelt lost the love of his life *and* his mother two days after his daughter was born—on the same fucking day—and just said "fuck it," ran off to North Dakota, became an epic cowboy, and then went on to become President.[36] He allowed his trauma to redefine him in a way many of us probably aren't even capable of. Look, sometimes shitty things just happen, and they are nothing other than shitty. But it's important to ask ourselves how the things that happen to us shape us. It's important when our own choices or circumstances take a wrong turn that we pay attention to the next direction we take. (Don't worry—no one expects you to become Teddy Roosevelt.)

The truth is, when fate or chance or God or whatever you wanna call it deals you a bad hand, it not only doesn't mean you're screwed, but it can actually make you better. Humans, as it turns out, are anti-fragile. We get stronger by getting hurt. When little kids fall down, they learn how to become better climbers. We have the capacity to thrive and grow the most during the hardest times in our lives. When faced with adversity or difficult situations, rather than whine about them, we have the opportunity to turn them into meaning-making experiences, the kind that force you to understand your world in a different way. They force you to look at yourself critically and wonder, *Where do I go from here? I no longer understand life in the way I once did, and I now have to reorganize my concepts to fit in this new puzzle piece.* When someone you love dies, or you lose your job, or your girlfriend

---

[36.] Wait, who was taking care of his newborn daughter?

dumps you—when you realize the way your parents treated you led to some legitimately fucked up behaviors as an adult—these are all meaning-making, paradigm-shifting opportunities.

Our brains are naturally inclined towards order. They like the predictable. They like to know what's going to happen because it's easier: you already have a response ready for this very familiar situation. But sometimes those automated responses your brain has built up are the wrong ones. When we encounter meaning-making situations, we are forced to reevaluate those well-worn neural pathways.

When you lose your job, you have the chance to truly think about what else you want to do. I mean really think about it. Getting fired can be the "blessing" that leads you to your next great opportunity. When a loved one dies, you can realize the value of so many things you were previously taking for granted. You can discover a new lease on life. When your best friend betrays you, you can find a way to forgive or learn a lesson about the kind of people you want to keep in your life.

And sometimes, the most terrible thing you can imagine happening is exactly what you needed to break you out of the rut you couldn't even see you were in. When I quit my job to be with a poet who never loved me and then got fired from my first waitressing gig and then some random dude drove my car into a pole, it ended up being the best string of terrible things that ever happened to me. Funny, huh?

Whether it's circumstances or choices—whether within our control or without—we're all going to find ourselves on the wrong path sometimes. We're all going to have to deal with shit that is hard, shit we didn't want, shit we didn't expect, shit we never saw coming. No matter how hard you try to follow the path you think is right for you, things are going to get in the way. Life is going to get in the way. Something about the best laid plans of mice and men.

The difference with the happy people in the world is they realize that no matter what it is, it's still okay. You're always okay because you've already made it through everything you've been through. And whatever you're going through now is already part of the new you who will exist tomorrow and every day after. The best we can do on our journey to finding our own happiness is to be willing to change course. To be willing to accept that sometimes things are fucked up. Sometimes life hands you lemons and you gotta make some motherfucking lemonade.

You can take the shitty things that happen to you in life and give up. You can say, "life is unfair," and then be miserable until you die. Or you can look to find another path in the rubble of everything you wanted. You can decide to be happy no matter what's happening.

You can decide to make some motherfucking lemonade.

january 2010

Four months have now passed since I left my life behind, and the fiery propulsion that launched me from Charlotte has flashed in sublimation to solid stone. The boy I loved, the car I loved, and the job I loved, burned to cinder in the heat of whatever it was that drove me here without a destination. I have four thousand dollars left. I am a shadow of myself again.

I do the only thing I know how to when I feel lost: get on Kayak and look up flights. I book the cheapest ticket I can to California. The urgency to leave DC rises in me as unrelenting as the need to leave Charlotte did, but this time, for all the wrong reasons. For a boy, for a sorrow, for an escape. I preach about letting the universe give you the right path, about letting it come as it should. Yet each step I force forward is on another land mine.

I sit on the plane to San Francisco and think of nothing but the poet. Of the reasons why I am flying to this city, his hometown, knowing he is here now. To my friends I say I just need to get out. I just need to think. It's not him, don't worry, I just want to explore California; I just want to visit sexy Danny, my ever friendly and charming fuck buddy from college. I've never been to San Francisco. Of course I'm not going to text the poet. Exploring the city alone, I am walking in his shadow; I am lying to myself.

The blithe winds of my free spirit were all a show, but who was it for? I was stupid to still love him, but more so to pretend I didn't, to feign insouciant and willfully ignore the decaying stench of what we were. I built a fortress of lace and prayed my bleary eyes not belie my carefully crafted facade. I was so sure that everything in DC was what I was supposed to have that I couldn't let go. There wasn't any other way. I had nothing else to hold on to. It had to be him; it had to be there. All of my friends, my freedom, everything I coveted in one small city, yet none of it made sense. DC was kicking me out.

The time I spend trying to forget about the poet with Danny is awkward and precarious as I poorly play my lighthearted part. He sees through every delicately conceived action, and I become an almost empty glass—nothing stirring around me but a few diluted memories of what used to burn inside. The fragile confidence I had spent so many years building is razed in a heartbeat. With the whole structure crumbling upon my tiny feet, I am seventeen again. Desperate and insecure. Pretending to be someone I'm not.

I have nothing left to lose, nothing left to look forward to, except a trip to New Zealand to spend the last of my money before I am left with less than nothing all over again. When my best friend calls to tell me the trip is canceled, I manage to spit out one struggled sentence, "I'm sorry love, I gotta go." I let the tears overwhelm me in Alamo Square.

And in that moment, my house of cards collapses. I'm not fooling anyone, and the universe was never buying it anyway. Nothing is right; this isn't what I need no matter how much I want it to be, and it is time to listen to something other than my own misguided desires. For the first time since I left Charlotte, I am honest with myself. In these moments when you think you have the least is when you always find the most.

When I get back to Danny's that evening, I prepare the same smile I had waiting for him before, but the pretense that had been exhausting me has dissolved. I confess the chaotic calamity of everything I wanted turning to dust—my job, my car, my love—what happened? Finally acquiescing to my broken self, I admit in earnest I have no idea what I am doing. And as if the universe had been watching, and waiting, for my inevitable confession, everything falls into place.

"Who cares if your friends can't go. Why don't you just move to New Zealand?"

And with Danny's nonchalant statement—yet another made in passing that would end up changing my life—the world opens itself up to me without a hurdle or a second thought, like a bridge that materializes with each step forward you take. And in turn, the woman I once knew myself to be effloresces from the shriveled bud to which I had withered. I found a way. I heard that voice again. I listened.

My working holiday visa is approved in a day. Within two days, I have a one-way ticket to Auckland. There is not a shred of doubt that what I am doing is what I am meant to be doing. The feeling is inextricable from me. I am at once bound to it and free because of it. I can never ignore it again.

from the inside out

the hedonic treadmill

I hope by now that some of you are thinking about quitting your job and running away. Exciting, isn't it!? Or maybe at the very least, you're learning how to view money as a means to an end rather than an end in itself. Hopefully you stopped buying clothes to improve your social status, and you stopped doing yoga and hanging out with fucking Linda. You're looking for a new job if you wanted one, starting your Etsy store full of vintage glassware, whatever. You're doing as many things as you can that will help you get to that elusive happy.

I mean, that's why we strive to meet our oughts and ideals, right? Whether internally or externally guided, it's because we want to be happy. Everybody wants to be happy. We create lives that we believe will bring us joy—whether the things we're doing will get the job done or not. You think buying that car will make you happy, and I think traveling will make me happy. Whether it comes from the right place or the wrong place, we're all trying to chase the same warm, fuzzy feeling on this wacky rock hurtling through space: happiness.

Maybe you want to move to Paris because you think that will make you happy. Or maybe you don't want to move anywhere. Maybe you're not desperately *un*happy, but you're floating through life feeling like you're barely living it. Is this what happiness is? Is this *all* there is? No matter where you live or what you do, you still have bills and groceries and TV shows and maybe kids or maybe not kids—you have these things in Paris and in Idaho and in New Zealand and living in a van down by the river. We still have to find a way to be happy in between all the other shit that occupies our lives. We can Marie Kondo the stuff and Marie Kondo our friends, but at some point, we gotta Marie Kondo the inside—the parts inside of us that don't spark joy.

If everything you're doing is in line with your authentic, ideal self, then you'll be happy right? Not so fast. Sorry to burst your bubble after all this talk of changing everything to live your most authentic life. No matter how many dreams you achieve, no matter how authentic and honorable and admirable your desires, if you're working from a list, it will never provide lasting happiness. Even if your goal is to cure cancer, and then you do it, it still doesn't guarantee happiness. Sometimes travel makes me happy for a moment, or a day, or a week, but it's not a state of being that you can achieve. It's not an end in itself any more than money or a flourishing career. Because once you get the thing you want, then what?

There was a study done a few years back (which I can't seem to find) that asked people to rate their own happiness over time, on a scale of 1 to 10. Most people, on average, would give themselves a 7. Not too shitty, not too ecstatic. Then, maybe you get a promotion and a raise, and you rate yourself a 9 for a little while. But the interesting part of the study was that over time, everyone ended up back at 7. The wonderful new apartment you got just becomes your regular apartment, and then you find something else to complain about.[37] The guy who went down to a 3 after he got fired went back up to a 7 too.

This is known as the "hedonic treadmill," a term coined in a popular 1978 study that tracked the happiness of lottery winners and accident victims who became paraplegics.[38] While

---

[37] If you've ever watched the show *Succession* you can get a nice glimpse at how meaningless fancy things are when you're a billionaire.

[38] Philip Brickman, Dan Coates, and Ronnie Janoff-Bulman, "Lottery winners and accident victims: Is happiness relative?" *Journal of Personality and Social Psychology*, 36(8), (1978): 917–927, https://psycnet.apa.org/record/1980-01001-001.

the amputees were ever-so-slightly less happy than the control group, the lottery winners weren't any happier *at all* than the control group. Certainly the feeling of winning the lottery was an ecstatic, life-altering high . . . until . . . it wasn't.

As soon as you achieve anything on your list, it becomes your status quo. As soon as you move into that mansion, you forget all about your studio apartment. This is the new status quo, and it fades into the background just like everything else. And then we start looking for new things that get us back up from a 7 to a 9. And herein lies the root of the problem: so long as you are looking for something else or waiting to attain something else in order to be happy, you will never be happy. Ouch.

The desire for a more positive experience is itself a negative experience. And, paradoxically, the acceptance of one's negative experience is itself a positive experience.

This is known as the Backwards Law concept, coined by modern philosopher Alan Watts (though it originated in Zen Buddhism), and made popular in Mark Manson's bestselling book, *The Subtle Art of Not Giving a F*ck*. Read that passage again. Only by accepting whatever your negative circumstances are can you find happiness. The desire in itself to have more positive experiences, to be happier, is a negative one because it is a thing you do not have. It feeds from your expectation-reality gap and leaves you wishing and wanting and unfulfilled. But as soon as you can accept all of the things in your life the way that they are, you realize that you already had the capacity for happiness. You realize that it doesn't come from finding a more positive experience, but from accepting the circumstances you have. I know that may sound easier said than done, but it just takes a moment of clarity. Maybe for me it was those happy, statistically impoverished children in the Cambodian rice paddies or living barefoot in Wanaka. Maybe for you it will be this book.

But if nothing we achieve or earn or have can provide us with lasting happiness—even if it's aligned with our authentic ideals—then what's the fucking point? Well, living more in line with who you are is a great start. Allowing yourself to put your unique self out into the world, to pursue the things that actually matter to you does make a difference. Achieving things that you're pursuing because they're meaningful, authentic goals will bring a much more lasting sense of satisfaction than mindlessly pursuing the things you're supposed to want—that society has told you you should want.

It just won't work every day. It can't. Because as soon as you start inhabiting the life you were meant to lead, the hedonic treadmill has you forgetting when you were working in that awful job wearing all those sweaters you sort of hated. So then how are we supposed to just *be* happy?

It's up to us to find it in the lives we already have and the people we love—whether we're living our authentic lives or still finding our way there. We can find happiness in a delicious meal or a lovely sunset or hugging our kids or just in being thankful for a roof and a bed. We have to find happiness in the things we already have, because there is literally nowhere else to find it. Any external desire for something we don't have causes a gap that makes us unhappy, and anything we do get will only snap us back on the hedonic treadmill right back to where we started while we start wishing for something else.

Pretty fucked up, huh?

But it's liberating at the same time. Because it means our happiness is always within our control. Once we understand that chasing all the things we've been chasing won't bring lasting happiness when we get them, we get to start being happy right fucking now.

And how do we do that after we leave our shitty jobs and our shitty husbands and stop hanging out with fucking Linda? By working to bring joy to ourselves and others. By looking around at our lives and deciding that there are things to be grateful for. If you're rich and have a gigantic mansion that the hedonic treadmill has made you take for granted, look around and appreciate it. If you're poor and share an apartment with three other dudes and none of you knows how to do the laundry, appreciate it. I'm sure there are things that suck about your life. That rich housewife has no real friends. Your bachelor pad smells like dirty gym socks. Neither of you has everything you want. Because you never can. There will never be a perfect period of your life. But then a few years go by, and you look back fondly at your smelly gym-sock apartment and think, *Man, those were the days!*

No matter what your goals are, how authentic your self-guides are, no matter how much you achieve everything you think you want to achieve, how much you're following the path you know you're meant to take, there isn't a version of your life that doesn't include suffering. Even when all of your needs are met, you will always find something to complain about. Things can never be perfect, and striving for perfection of any kind—attaching your happiness to something you're working towards—is a surefire way to be miserable your whole life.

Every period of our lives, every place we live, every thing we do has room for gratitude and room for joy. You are the only person who is getting in the way of that. Happiness is a choice. It's one we make every day. It's something we bring into our own lives or we don't. Nothing and no one can give it to you. But you can help to give it to someone else, which is one of the best ways to get it right back in return.

Joy doesn't exist in the world, it exists in us.

—*Ben Franklin*

high-hanging fruit

Are you happy yet? Did reading that last chapter unlock rainbows of joy shooting from every orifice of your body? Do little cartoon birds help you get dressed in the morning now? I didn't think so. Starting to understand that the things we want aren't going to make us happy—even if they're valuable and authentic ideals—is a crucial step in the process. The next step is to start making the small choices, the each-and-every-day choices, to help bring joy to yourself and others. We have to take the things inside of ourselves that are clouding our thoughts with negativity and erase them. We have to work from the inside out.

Most of what we talked about in the second section was related to esteem: the internal esteem we get from meeting our own goals and the external esteem we get from friends, and colleagues, and women who compliment our shoes at bus stops. But there is another level in Maslow's hierarchy, the highest level: self-actualization. Once we have all the esteem we need from all the different sources, whatever they are, we naturally start to work on ourselves. We just get up one day and decide we want to be the best versions of ourselves we can be! We decide there's more to life than money and careers and whatever else . . . at least I think that's how it works? You're reading this book anyway, right?

So how do we get to this elusive self-actualization, and what is it even? Maslow breaks it down into a few different parts. The first is acceptance and realism: self-actualized people have an honest, accurate perception of who they are and where they fit in the world around them. They recognize their own faults and strengths. Without this realism, you will experience cognitive dissonance, which we'll talk about more in a minute. The next is problem-centering. Self-actualized people have transcended the need for internal gain. Once you realize that it won't make you happy anyway, you can focus your efforts on things that will improve the community and the world around you rather than your own circumstances. You make decisions based on empathy. Because of the increased honesty and empathy, self-actualized people have an increased capacity for deep and loving relationships with others. And on top of it all, self-actualized people have an increased ability for peak experiences—transcending experiences of wonder, joy, awe, and creativity. Maslow describes them as "rare, exciting, oceanic, deeply moving, exhilarating, elevating experiences that generate an advanced form of perceiving reality, and are even mystic and magical in their effect upon the experimenter."[39]

Sounds pretty great, huh?

Unfortunately, not everyone will become self-actualized. Plenty of people will live their lives running on esteem, filling the void with one thing and the next, and that's it. There's nothing inherently wrong with that; it doesn't mean you're a terrible person. But if we want to at least try—if we want to be the best versions of ourselves we can be—then we need to clean out the cobwebs of negative paradigms that have been directing our actions for so long. We need to hit the reset button and start questioning what kind of people we've been and what kind of people we want to be. We need to be honest about who we've been up to this point, no matter how hard it is to do. We have to strive towards the ideals that Maslow laid out—honesty, empathy, selflessness, deep and loving relationships—in order to get to the best that life has to offer, in order to experience true happiness.

What pieces of this do you think you're missing now? When

---

[39]. Abraham Maslow, "Religious aspects of peak-experiences," In Sadler, W.A. (ed.), *Personality and Religion*. (New York: Harper & Row, 1970).

you think about your ideal self, what's left on your list? Or did you maybe add a whole bunch of things to your list a second ago? When you think about the important relationships in your life, do you feel like they are based in deep honesty and empathy? This isn't an easy question to answer, especially if you don't have any truly healthy relationships to use as a compass. So think about it. Think about your husband and your mom and your brother and your best friend. What was the last interaction you had with them? How are most of your interactions with them? Have you been coming from a place of honesty and authenticity? If so, are the people in your life willing to receive and reciprocate it?

Everyone who is in your life, who means something to you, who holds an important role, has to be open and honest and care about you as a person. And you have to be and do the same. If you're still making decisions to please other people, you have to ask yourself if those people give a shit about you. If you're no longer the person who is trying to be rich and well-connected and well-dressed, do those people still care about you? Are they supporting you on your journey? The people who truly care about you don't care about your money or your car or your clothes. They just want you to be happy. And anyone who does care about those things, doesn't truly care about you. And as long as you keep hanging out with those people, you're going to keep beating yourself up for not having enough, for not being attractive or successful or charming enough.

Until all of the choices you make with other people are rooted in having honest, vulnerable, and authentic relationships, you're going to feel stuck, stalled, and dissatisfied. Only through honesty and vulnerability can you forge real relationships. And it might be hard. You might lose a lot of friends and burn a lot of bridges when you realize how many of your relationships were some kind of mutually beneficial agreement between two semi-shitty people.

If you're scared of losing the shitty friends you have, don't be. There are enough wonderful, authentic people in the world who won't judge you for these things, who are just trying to be happy and want everyone around them to be happy too, whatever that looks like. I promise. And once you start putting only honesty back out into the world, the relationships you create will be the kind that can withstand anything. Because they're real.

In order to do that, however, we're going to have to do some hard work. We're going to have to take an honest look at the things that are making us unhappy—whether it's our attitudes or our relationships. If happiness can only come from within yourself, then that's the first place we need to look.

The good news is that once you get through these hard parts, the rest of everything is so much easier. The background noise of work and groceries and bills can become just that—background noise. When you're able to focus on the relationships that matter, on becoming a better person for yourself and others, on appreciating the wonderful things about the things you already have, your perspective on everything changes. You can still be happy while cleaning fucking toilets.

Everything here may not apply to you, but I urge you not to gloss over it believing that you're doing just fine. It's not easy to truly look in the mirror, and we all have something we can stand to learn about ourselves and the way we interact with all those other humans we keep seeing every day. Life is relationship—it is the core of everything, the reason we are, the thing that makes us happy in the here and now, the thing we desire most after food, shelter, and clothing: belonging. So how do we do that? How do we do that in the best way possible? If self-actualization means becoming the best version of ourselves that there is, where the hell do we start?

becoming translucent

Nine years ago, while sitting around a table in Seoul, South Korea, my incredibly introspective friend Matthew suggested we play a game. He said, "Let's all go around the table and say the worst thing we think about everyone."

Fun game.

I volunteered to be the first one to go. One by one, people told me my biggest flaw. And when I say "one by one," I mean only Matthew said anything because everyone immediately agreed with his assessment:

"You're pretty abrasive."

At the age of twenty-nine, it had never even occurred to me that I was abrasive. I used to be incredibly sarcastic in college, which I toned down after many people warned me of how harsh it was. I thought I was just loud and funny. Turns out that "loud and funny" to me meant "loud and rude and too blunt and curses too much" to other people. It hadn't crossed my mind I was being offensive. I honestly thought I was a hilarious human being. Maybe it was the years I spent living on Long Island where everyone is loud and curses too much and tells both friends and strangers to casually go fuck themselves. Maybe it was my year in New Zealand where calling someone a "good cunt" is a compliment.

Wherever it came from, I struggled immensely with this concept: if I stop being sarcastic because people don't like it, then I'm not being true to myself anymore. But if the point of my sarcasm was to be a joke, and it was actually hurting people's feelings and having the opposite effect, then why would I insist on behaving that way?

I don't think Matthew was ever personally offended by me or my abrasiveness (at least I hope not), but his statement jarred me all the same. People thought I was rude. This was a way that I was. This was part of the list of traits people would assign to me.

Maybe it's because I couldn't imagine seeing my behavior as wrong when it came from the right place. We all want to be liked; we all want to have friends. How could someone misconstrue my hilarious joke as an insult? But they did. And they do. And it's because we're all vastly different humans. It's because my bone-dry sarcasm comes off as an insult to some people. It's because someone's well-meaning advice comes off as condescending to another. As much as you may think you are who you think you are, the real truth is that the way your actions are perceived by others means far more for your relationships in the world than your intentions.

There is an Italian book, which translated into English is titled *One, None and a Hundred-thousand*,[40] where the main character realizes that there are as many different versions of him in the world as people he has met—and none of them is the same as the person he sees himself as. Who he is to his best friend is different than the perception of who he is to the man at the coffee shop he chats with every day. Every person you know and meet creates their own idea of who you are within the constructs that they have built up to categorize people over time. And yes, we all categorize people; our brains simply don't work any other way. So I had created an idea of who I was in my head, but then discovered it wasn't aligned with the woman that my friends saw me to be. But what does it mean if the authentic person you thought you were presenting to other people isn't the person they were seeing?

As I dug a little deeper into Matthew's comment, the rest

[40.] There is a free English translation of the book available here, at the Gutenberg Project: http://gutenberg.net.au/ebooks16/1600681h.html#ch01-04.

of the table slowly chimed in in agreement. Yes, you curse too much. You're too loud. You don't have a filter. You're just *out there*. Sometimes you say mean things. Okay. Good to know. I have a lot of things to think about.

And now it was Matthew's turn. What was his worst quality? The table sat in silence as we contemplated what somewhat negative, yet hopefully constructive thing to say.

"You're a little neurotic about cleaning things?" I suggested.

"Yeah, you're like, super clean—to a fault." My future husband agreed.

"So *nothing* serious?" Matthew added incredulously.

"No, I mean, you're just generally a really nice guy. I mean, you've never said or done anything mean or rude or selfish. You're maybe too obsessed with other people's opinions of you though?"

I guess I was the only one with such an obvious flaw to point out.

So on that night, I learned I was abrasive. I learned that lots of people agreed with that assessment even though it was something I never meant to be. And I saw a choice I had to make. I could decide to become more demure in my late twenties. I could decide that this label was not a label I wanted to wear for the rest of my life. Or, I could decide that I spent long enough figuring out who I was and that spending another decade pretending to be a nice, quiet girl wasn't on the docket.

But in that light, what does it mean to become translucent and own your faults while somehow remaining authentic? How do we find the line between being the person we think we are and the person the world sees us as? How do we become better without sacrificing who we are? Paradigm shift alert!

After a lot of uncomfortable soul-searching, I came to the first conclusion that not everyone has to like me. While we're at it, you should probably also come to that conclusion, right now. No matter who you are or what you do, some people aren't going to like you. It's not just part of being some aberrant flouter of society; it's part of being any human. We all like different things and different music and different art and different kinds of people. Whether you're nice or cynical or funny or rebellious, some people just aren't gonna be into that. And that's okay.

But while everyone doesn't have to like me, at the very least, my internal concept of my actual self should be aligned with the actual self that the world sees. I had to synthesize this new information with my own self-image. I had to accept that I was abrasive, recognize the times in my life that this was potentially hurting people I care about, and—if I wanted to become a better person—stop fucking doing that. I had to find that difficult line between being myself and being the person I want to put out into the world. So I thought long and hard about the times that maybe I had said something that I never meant to be hurtful but had ended up coming off that way to other people. I tried to see myself through my friends' perceptions rather than my own intentions. I tried to fix the parts that were shitty while keeping the parts that were me.

This may come as a massive surprise, but I've never been able to hide things. I was born with the lack of a capacity that nearly everyone else seems to possess to just keep their feelings to themselves. If I don't tell people how I feel, I explode. This unfiltered honesty has more than once been a problem. Dare I say . . . it can be a bit abrasive. Not only do I offend people, but I lack delicacy in sensitive situations. A very close friend once confided in me that he was having suicidal thoughts. I told him, "Don't be ridiculous, of course you're not going to kill yourself." Needless to say, though this was my honest opinion and was possibly true, it wasn't what he needed to hear in that moment.

There are certainly times for my unfiltered honesty, but that was not one of those times. And it reminds me all the time that I need to be careful with those I love; I need to consider where they're coming from and where they are in each vulnerable moment—especially in their vulnerable moments. We need to ask ourselves in every situation, is it better to be honest or to be kind? Or as Rule #1 of my shared house rules after college said: don't be a dick.

I make a point for my jarring honesty—which can often be harsh to the person on the receiving end—to come from the right place. For it to come from a place where I'm trying to help my friends understand a little more about themselves, to challenge them and make them better. Not just to say something rude under the guise of being authentic.

My abrasiveness is seen as a fault by a lot of people I meet, I'm sure. I think I rub more people the wrong way than the right one. But at the end of the day, I decided it's okay to be abrasive sometimes so long as I'm not hurting the people who matter to me. I have found a few friendly souls who like (or perhaps tolerate) my loud, curse-filled political rants, and appreciate at the very least, the humor and sometimes brutal honesty that come with me. Now that I know that my true actual self is often seen as abrasive, I can make a choice about when that's appropriate and to what to degree.

I know I have to play interview Taylor and grown-up-cocktail-party Taylor and someone's-kids-are-in-the-room Taylor (though that Taylor has to come out much more often than I care for these days). I push boundaries in these situations, but mostly within reason (I hope). Generally speaking, as often as I can to the fullest extent that I can, I let myself be myself. I drink and smoke and say what I think; I make sometimes crude (yet hilarious) jokes, and I say everything too loudly (not on purpose, this is just how my voice is; you can hear my laugh three states over). And I try not to hurt people's feelings along the way. And even with all this intense self-awareness, I still say things that I think are funny and other people are like, "Damn. That was way harsh, Tai."

I'm not saying these are all great qualities to have, but they are mine. I've been too loud and boisterous and bouncing off the walls since I was a kid. All those years I was stifling those parts of me were years that I hated. So I made a choice that as long as the people who actually matter to me don't think I'm being an asshole, I'm okay with some randos at a cocktail party thinking I'm a little inappropriate.

On that note, let's play a fun new version of Matthew's game. List all of the worst things you can think about yourself. I'll go first:

> *Too abrasive*
> *Stubborn*
> *Too loud, curses too much*
> *Can be insensitive to people's feelings*
> *Overly critical of myself*
> *Overly critical of everything*
> *Complains too much*
> *Doesn't give people a chance*
> *Doesn't easily forgive others*
> *Often selfish*

There, that wasn't so hard (just kidding, I've spent the last nine years contemplating that list, and it was still rough). Recognizing our own faults (and then admitting them out loud) is not something that comes naturally to any of us. Most of us are trying to be as close as possible to that list we made back in the first section. We have admirable traits that we hope people see in us, and we tend to sort of gloss over the rest. We will go to unimaginable lengths to see our own behavior through rose-colored glasses. It's easier that way. We give ourselves the benefit of every doubt because coming to terms with the fact that maybe you've been a shitty, self-involved person is, well, shitty. But we all have flaws. And being able to look yourself in the mirror honestly is one of the hardest things for us to do.

Things are opaque to us, and we are opaque to ourselves.

We don't want to admit that we were wrong or see ourselves in a negative light. We don't want to admit that we may be the villain in someone else's story. And I promise you, you *are* the villain in someone else's story. We can look at the behavior of another and judge it as jealousy, selfishness, or laziness but see the same behavior in ourselves as completely justified. *I'm not lazy, I'm selectively motivated. I'm not selfish, I just need to look out for myself right now.* We are masters of rationalization. We ramble endlessly about our own problems, but never listen. We don't forgive but expect to be forgiven. We build towers of slights against us, remembering every transgression without remembering that everyone is dealing with their own shit, without considering what could be going on in someone else's life.

Every person you see has an entire world of pain and worry and joy and everything else running inside their own head, the same movie we all play for ourselves. We are the stars of our own shows, the centers of our own universes. We are incompetent and judgmental in the same moment. We are riddled with anxiety or overcome with obsessive tendencies. And while all of these behaviors are "part" of who we are now—the person that has been created over so many years on this earth—it doesn't mean they're part of being authentic.

If we're going to become better people, we have to be honest with ourselves. Authenticity requires that honesty. You can easily say "this is who I am, I am being myself. This is the authentic me." And maybe that's true. You should be you and no one else, but shouldn't you be the best you you can be? "Not giving a fuck" and "doing whatever the fuck you want" can become heinous behaviors when they disregard the feelings (note the difference between feeling and judgments) of others around you.

If all this second guessing and self-introspection is starting to sound counterintuitive to doing whatever you want and not giving a fuck what people think, let me clarify a key piece of the puzzle. Stop giving a fuck what shitty people think: the people who are judging you for what kind of car you drive, the people who scoff at your outfit or make you feel bad about yourself or cock their head sympathetically to the side when you tell them you're a garbage man. The only person those thoughts are trying to hurt is you. But you should give a fuck if you're hurting someone. Start caring about the people and things *that matter*.

When you're looking at your list of all the worst things about you, ask yourself, *Are these things that hurt people I care about? Are these things I want to change about myself?*

I've already talked about being abrasive, about trying to take that honesty that could be so hurtful and turn it into something productive without giving up who I am. And I think I've made progress over the years (someone call me out if I'm being delusional here). But the biggest one I'm working on these days is being selfish. I like being the center of attention; I like telling a funny story when I'm out with friends and making people laugh. And sometimes, I don't listen as much as I wait for my turn to talk. I'm sure a lot of us do.

I want to be less selfish. I want to remember, when my friend complains about that guy at work, to check back in the following week. I want the people I love to know that I love and care about them. It doesn't always come naturally to me like it does for some people I know, so I work to do that. I work to listen better because that is a trait I think is valuable. That is the person I want to cultivate within me. That is the authentic ideal self I am working to align with. Sometimes I mess up and forget all about that guy at work.

When I confessed this to some of the friends I've made in the last year, they were honestly surprised to hear that I thought about myself as selfish. So maybe, just maybe, working on that part of me has actually been working! We should all be growing and changing constantly, reconsidering ourselves and our place in the world and working to become better. If we're healthy individuals, our ideal selves should always be separate from our actual selves. Because when we stop growing, we become complacent. When we become complacent, we stop caring, and we revert back to living in a fog, feeling unfulfilled, and stuffing that void with things and TV and complaining about being too busy or too bored all the time. Or you'll just end up in a bunch of unhealthy relationships with other emotionally-stunted people.

Look, I know I said you can do whatever the fuck you want, and you can. You don't have to grow if you don't want to. You don't have to be less selfish or more kind or anything else. But if you're a miserable, whining, cynical, sanctimonious dickhead who goes around judging and hating everyone and everything, don't be surprised when people don't really enjoy your company. And FYIsies, this is usually a personality that is cultivated as a defense mechanism to avoid being hurt or shunned: reject everything before it has a chance to reject you.

Liking something makes us vulnerable to ridicule, for example, loving the *Twilight* books even though you're a forty-year-old man or taking bubble baths if you're a man of any age. It can feel embarrassing to like a thing that society has deemed uncool or unmanly, and many of us—even fully grown adults—will downplay our "guilty pleasures" such as being into the same music as your teenage daughter. But then all of a sudden, you may find yourself defined by all the things you hate. *This band is awful; that restaurant is the worst; you actually like that show?* Criticizing both things and people puts us above them in our minds. It protects us from them. It is why kids bully other kids and why teenage girls (and fully grown adult women) ostracize other women. Negativity and exclusion are somehow ingrained at the core of "being cool."

And yet, as an adult, the happiest people are the ones who like the most things. The happiest people are the ones who can find joy no matter what they're doing—the ones who scream along to Taylor Swift with the windows down while stuck in traffic. The happiest people are the ones who don't give a fuck what other people think about their taste in music—the ones who don't give a fuck what other people think about almost anything. And not only that, but the happiest, most positive people who go about their day with blindly happy energy shooting from their eyeballs . . . are the most-liked people! It's infectious!

For the record, I am not one of those people, and you don't have to be either. Some of my best friends are cynics, and I think their deadpan criticisms are hilarious. I'm sure a lot of people they meet on this planet disagree. If you want to stop being so negative because you think it's making you unhappy or ruining your relationships, then work to get more positive. But if you like being a cynic, and the people in your life love your wonderful, cynical self, then keep on keeping on. There are no right or wrong answers, only right and wrong reasons, only right and wrong outcomes. You be you, boo.

I want to be a more positive person; I want the people I love to think I'm a positive person, and by all accounts I should be one. I am positive in a lot of ways, in the love I share with my husband and my friends, in the unrestrained laughter I release into the world. But I also end up complaining without realizing it. I am naturally critical and analytical; I like to deconstruct things in order to understand them. In my head that sounds totally normal, but to other people maybe it sounds like I am a miserable cunt who complains about everything. Even my husband can't tell the difference sometimes. He thinks I am unhappy until I explain to him that I can criticize aspects of a thing without *feeling* negative about it. Right? Right???? If I don't realize I'm being negative, and I don't intend to be negative, then am I? Or is everyone else just misunderstanding me, and it's their fault?

And now we're right back at the beginning again! In the quest to find authenticity within ourselves and share it with the world, this'll really cook your noodle. My nature is to be critical of things and to dissect them. I don't know another way to be (trust me, I've tried). But I don't want to be perceived as a negative person because that means I'm bringing negativity into the world. If I stop being loud and witty and sarcastic, I'm not being me, but I still don't want to hurt other people or have people think I'm a raging bitch. So what the fuck are you supposed to do???

Figure it out. Start doing that deep dive we all need to do into what kind of people we want to be—into what matters to us each the most. Start becoming translucent. It may sound like I am contradicting myself or providing confusing, impossible advice. And I am. Nothing in this world is black or white or all good or all bad. Everything we are and do and say is nuanced. There is no one answer to everything; everything is give and take. Our brains strive so hard to make things simple, to compartmentalize everything, and we have to actively work against that.

I need to find a better line to draw with my criticism if I don't want to be so negative. I need to frame the things I say in a different way; I need to work harder to stay in the moment rather than deconstruct it. Maybe you need to start setting boundaries with your friends who walk all over you, but it doesn't mean never doing someone another favor. We have to think. We have to break out of the easy patterns that we have etched into our neural pathways and fight to find the right answers. We have to look critically at ourselves and say, *Hey, maybe I could be better, but I still want to keep this part of who I am.* And that's okay.

We must make every effort we can to look in the mirror and think, *How can I get closer to the ideal me I want to be?* And honestly, just that act every day can provide a meaning in your life that maybe you've been lacking. When you start to see that you can change your behavior, that you can be a little nicer to your neighbor and they suddenly reciprocate. When you see that when you stop complaining so much about work or your husband or traffic that it breaks you out of a rut . . . that everything just starts to feel better.

As much as we have the choice to change our jobs or our clothes or our apartments, we have the choice to change at least parts of our personalities. We have the choice to cultivate positive behavior and recognize our flaws when we exhibit them. We have the choice to try to get better, even if sometimes we still fall victim to those same tendencies.

Put all that energy you used to put into living up to some imaginary ideal and start putting it towards becoming the best version of you you can be. Ask your friends to be brutally honest with you. Think about all the thoughts that run through your head each day . . . how many are negative? What about the words coming out of your mouth? How often do you criticize rather than praise? How often do you really listen to other people or just wait for your turn to talk? Hear the things you have spent your entire life trying not to hear. And actually listen this time.

I can promise you right now, you won't completely fix your flaws. If you tend to be selfish, or jealous of your friends' success, or impatient, or unkind, or judgmental, or whatever it is, those will probably stay with you a long time. You have been living your whole life this way, and it is so very hard to undo the years of well-worn neural pathways that have led us to the people we have become. But recognizing them (cliché alert!) is the hardest part. Knowing is half the battle; admitting you have a problem is the first step . . . you get the idea.

Once you are willing to admit that you have these faults, you can start to see them more and more in your daily life and interactions. You can recognize that jealousy when it comes up and question it. You can notice when you're being a little short with your husband and try to exercise a little more patience. And when the people who are close to you are doing the same things—when they are being harsh or unkind or controlling or whatever else—tell them. But just try to do it kindly. It isn't rocket science. We should all be trying to be better humans, and getting better takes work. You won't stop caring what people think about you overnight, but you can recognize that feeling when it comes up and question it. You can feel when you're about to lose your temper, and maybe, just maybe, not fly off the handle this time.

Becoming translucent is hard fucking work. If you really can't come up with a list of your faults or things you want to improve about yourself, try asking a group of friends after having a couple drinks. They'll be more than happy to chime in! Just don't bite their heads off when they do. Watch for the reaction in your body as you hear things you definitely don't want to hear. Watch how quickly your brain rejects any negative information that doesn't align with your concept of yourself. Watch how quickly you come to your own defense and start explaining away the things they bring up. Then fight that. See yourself from someone else's perspective.

Once you have your list, however you've arrived at it, I want you to think hard about each thing on it. Ask yourself, does this hurt other people? Is this hurting myself? Is this in line with who I thought I was or who I want to be?

We are all works in progress. None of us is ever finished. The best we can do is work to become less opaque to ourselves. And to remember that everyone on this planet is broken in some way, just like we are.

undrama your llamas

Reading this chapter won't be easy if you're doing it right. Even if you have wonderful friends who are willing to sit around a table and tell you all the worst things about yourself, it can still be nearly impossible for us to accept them. We just aren't programmed to do it.

Cognitive dissonance theory[41] states that when presented with information that contradicts our views (whether our views on politics or our views on who we are as people), we literally double down on being wrong rather than change our minds. It's fighting against all of our human nature to admit when we are wrong just one time in one argument. We'll end a friendship with a person who calls us out for something before we ever admit we made a mistake. We'll rationalize the behavior or seek out information from another source that confirms what we originally thought. Now think about admitting you've been wrong every day, for years . . . about yourself. None of us is immune to this thinking, and yet none of us is without fault.

Most of us dismiss the term "drama" as something that happens on Real Housewives of Orange County; most of us dismiss toxicity as a blatantly abusive relationship without realizing how many more subtle and insidious ways these things can creep into our own relationships, into the subtle ways we speak

---

[41]. Leon Festinger, Henry Riecken, and Stanley Schachter, *When Prophecy Fails: A Social and Psychological Study of a Modern Group That Predicted the Destruction of the World*, (Harper-Torchbooks, January 1956).

to and interact with our friends, colleagues, and families. If you get to the end of this chapter and think, *I definitely don't do any of those things*, try again. We can all be better people. But first we have to be willing to admit what we've been doing wrong.

>>>>>>>>>>>>>

One day in college, I was hanging out with Dan and the rest of the hippies, long after the bright blue pants incident. I was telling some story about getting a flat tire or running out of gas, or something else shitty that happened to me. As I finished, one of the guys responded, "Man, you really complain a lot." I couldn't believe it. I hadn't felt like I was complaining at all really, just telling a story of a thing that happened. I wasn't necessarily looking for pity or trying to be negative. I had no idea that was the personality I was projecting into the world. That was one of the last times I ever hung out with those guys (for totally unrelated reasons), but the comment stuck with me for the rest of my life.

Shortly after that, I read a book called *The Celestine Prophecy* that changed my whole perspective on shit. In this book, which is not at all a self-help book but rather a New Age exploration into spirituality and collective consciousness wrapped in an adventure novel with a valuable lesson on interpersonal relationships, they talk about the energy between people. Every interaction you have, energy is being exchanged between you and the other person. In unhealthy interactions, someone is "stealing" the energy in one way or another in order to boost themselves up. The book lays out four archetypes for unhealthy exchanges of energy and calls them control dramas.

On that particular day in college, I was telling Dan and the boys a story about how my car broke down, and they were listening intently and sending me their *Oh poor thing, how terrible* energy. I was sucking up other people's energy by complaining all the time. It's a trap I still have to consciously avoid, one

I already mentioned in the last chapter. This type of control drama is known as the "Poor Me." You gain your energy by getting people to feel bad for you. In more manipulative examples, you might be used to saying things like "It's fine, I'll just do it, I'm used to doing everything by myself." The guilt trip is the weapon of choice for the "Poor Me." While *The Celestine Prophecy* is about as pseudosciencey as you can get, these control dramas are based on a popular psychology book published in 1964 called *Games People Play*. Eric Berne's original book laid out a wealth of daily interactions that we all engage in, some healthy, some not-so-healthy.

At the core of our interactions, all of us, in one way or another, are looking for reassurances from others that they love us and care for us or that we're worthwhile and important. Berne calls these reassurances "strokes." The more accumulated negative encounters we have in our childhoods, the more we need to make up for that as adults, the more desperate we become for love and attention—to collect those strokes in our daily interactions. While there are a lot of nice, healthy ways to get strokes referred to by Berne as rituals or pastimes (chatting with neighbors or friends or spouses about this or that), the unhealthy interactions we have are referred to as games. A game, by Berne's own definition, contains an ulterior motive, whether conscious or not.

To illustrate the nature of these ulterior motives, he presents a game called "If It Weren't For You," commonly played in many (fucked up) marriages in the 1950s apparently. In this particular version, the wife frequently laments how many things she'd be able to do if it weren't for her overbearing husband, when in reality, she is actually too scared to do these things and secretly enjoys being controlled by him. She makes him feel bad for taking away her freedom, and so, because he's nice and loves her, he does her more favors to make up for it. She's manipulating additional strokes from him. She also gets the added benefit of being able to complain about him to her girlfriends, yet another game 1950s housewives engage in ("If It Weren't For Him").

Despite the often upsettingly out-of-touch examples in Berne's book, the psychoanalytic theory that supports all of this is still widely accepted. It's known as transactional analysis, where social interactions that we engage in to get different types of strokes or validation are categorized based on the ego states of the communicators. In every interaction, you're acting parent-like (nurturing or controlling), child-like (cooperative, resistant, spontaneous, or immature), or adult-like (objective and rational; unclouded by the ego states that your parents instilled in you). The four control dramas align with these ego states. If most of your interactions in life are characterized by both people being "adult-like," congratulations. That is 100 percent the idea. Which of the ego states we tend to defer to—whichever rituals or pastimes or games we tend to play—has a whole lot to do with how we got those strokes growing up. *The Celestine Prophecy* also covers a lot about which type of control dramas you're more likely to use based on what kind of people your parents were, so keep an eye out for repeating patterns as you start looking at your relationships.

Imagine you're at a party sitting with a large group of people. You think of something interesting to say and can't wait to share it, but when there is finally a lull in the conversation and you start talking, someone else just talks over you. You're being ignored. You immediately feel embarrassment as you were forced to trail off the sentence you had been waiting to say. You look to your left and right, but no one is paying attention to you. You've been denied the validation you were seeking. In the moments just after, depending on how you're feeling and who you are, you either shrugged it off as not a big deal (adult), blamed yourself for not being assertive enough (child), or got mad at everyone else for not listening to you (parent).

In Berne's book, he lays out the specific dynamics of dozens of these games and gives them hilariously specific names like "Why Does This Always Happen to Me" (WAHM – This is definitely one I am guilty of) and "Now I've Got You, You Son of a Bitch" (NIGYSOB – where you gleefully look for injustices and shortcomings in others and then point them out so you get to play the scolding parent). In my complaining example, I was playing a game of WAHM, acting like an immature child, and looking for the people in my life to take on the parental role of soothing and caring. I just didn't realize that's what I was doing to get the attention and validation I needed.

And therein lies the one major pitfall of transactional analysis as a therapeutic tool: it requires we have enough self-awareness to see that we're doing it. It requires our own translucence. For me, *The Celestine Prophecy* was the first book that helped me get there. It allowed me to start seeing my actions from outside of myself, to look at the relationships in my life from both sides. It was the first glimpse of translucence I had (paradigm shift alert!). If it takes that book or this book or Eric Berne's book or therapy or astrology to get you there, I don't care. You just gotta get there.

The other thing to recognize as we start to dig deeper into to these different games, control dramas, and ego states is that you don't have to be a terrible person to act terribly sometimes. You don't have to have diagnosed anger management issues to lose your temper. You don't have to be a sociopath to interact with your spouse and children and friends in mildly manipulative ways. We all play these games in one way or another whether we realize it or not. There is no shortage of the ways we perpetuate negative relationships and paradigms with those around us.

We get trapped in co-dependent patterns where we do favors for other people needing their praise for how wonderful we are, then get mad when they don't provide it—even though they never asked for the favor in the first place. We lack boundaries for ourselves, never saying no, never asserting ourselves because we were never taught to value our own time or opinions, but then we complain that we do too much for everyone. In the most disturbing game I read about in Berne's book, "Schlemiel," you fuck up someone else's shit, spilling drinks and burning cigarette holes in their furniture with the expectation of their forgiveness, and if they forgive you, you get that stroke, but even if they don't forgive you, you get to be mad at them for not forgiving you, so it's a win-win either way. What the actual fuck? Do people actually do this?

Despite being another seemingly absurd example, this game can be broken down to a destructive-child/forgiving-parent dynamic. The person burning holes in the couch could be anyone doing a destructive thing to other people in their lives and awaiting the forgiveness they know they should get. They are asking the other people in their lives to become the parent and treat them like a child. If the other person doesn't offer them that forgiveness because they are a healthy adult and they are fed up with this shit, the destructive child gets mad and tells them they're being a shitty friend. While Berne's games don't always align exactly with the four control dramas (some games can switch from one ego state to another), they all see us regressing to either a parent state or child state, away from the rational adults we are all capable of being.

Aside from the "Poor Me," the other predominately child-based control drama is "the Aloof." By pulling away from people and acting more mysterious and reserved, those who are aloof draw people in. You ask more questions, try to be there for them, and they only pull further away. I'm pretty sure this was the poet's entire personality, leading me to believe he was some incredibly mysterious and sexy man instead of just an insecure dick with poor grammar trying to be cool just like the rest of us. This control drama can also manifest in those annoyingly cryptic posts on Facebook that someone "doesn't want to talk about it" begging for people to respond with loving support. Or maybe your SO has asked you if anything is wrong and you say, "Nothing, I'm fine" in that voice that they 100 percent know means you are not at all fine? Yeah, I'm guilty of that one too. If you pull away from people in order to protect yourself, you may gain some emotional energy as people vie for you to open up to them, but you will never get to experience the full spectrum of honest human connection.

One of the fun aloof games you can play is "Why Don't You—Yes But" (YDYB). This is when people consistently offer solutions to the problem you're complaining about, but you just keep offering reasons why those solutions aren't good enough. Of course, you're not actually looking for solutions; the purpose of this interaction is to reassure or gratify your inner child. The people in the room offering solutions are existing solely for the benefit of the complainer, and you get to reject them again and again. They get to play the parent game of "I'm Only Trying to Help You." However, if someone actually does happen to offer a good solution, it can snap you out of the child state and into adult state. Oh shit, I think I might do this one too.

The next control drama on the list, which isn't one of my go-to faults, but is one by which I have been personally victimized, is "the Interrogator." The Interrogator steals energy by using questions that make people feel inferior, such as "Have you thought about going on a diet?" or "Aren't you cold in that short skirt?" These veiled criticisms will chip away at your confidence, often under the guise of helpfulness. A version that Berne refers to is called "Sweetheart." You say something kind of fucked up, but in a really nice way so that the other person can't call you out. If they do, you can just say you didn't mean anything by it; it was an innocent comment. See every movie trope of the overbearing mother-in-law. Think about your friends or your boyfriend or your husband . . . have you ever made one of these subtle digs? I'll let you guess which parent-child state this is.

The worst and most damaging by far of all the control drama types, however, is "the Intimidator." The Intimidator gains their energy by making other people feel inferior. When we are young, these are the bullies in school, but as we grow older, the paradigm doesn't change much, only the contexts. An intimidator drama can be any relationship where you're made to feel small. It encompasses the vast majority of truly toxic behavior that exists in relationships.

Maybe when your girlfriend tells you she's upset, you dismissively tell her she's overreacting, and she needs to grow up. You make her feel small by invalidating her feelings. Maybe you go one step further and gaslight her, denying you ever did or said what she's upset about in the first place, making her feel like she's crazy. Or maybe when you get angry you blame your partner, "Look what you did, you made me get so mad!" In Berne's book, this game is referred to as "See What You Made Me Do" (SWYMD). Another variation is "You Got Me Into This" where you let someone else make the decision so the blame isn't on you, but then get mad if they choose something that you don't end up liking.

Or maybe you're guilty of playing "Blemish?" When you meet a new person do you often immediately find a fault with them? This game starts in a child pity state of telling yourself you're not good enough—until you figure out what's wrong with the other person. Then you can turn them away. Reject them before they reject you. You become the parent-intimidator saying, "They're no good, I'm better than that." And that gives you control in the situation. The Intimidator needs to have control over the other person—this is where they get their energy.

The most outwardly apparent and damaging form of the Intimidator is of course, physical violence. An intimidator may just threaten violence in a relationship, or they may follow through on it. An Intimidator takes by force and likely grew up in a home where there was no other way to get attention. I'd venture to say you may know if you are an Intimidator, and I'd venture further to say you will need more help than a book to break the negative paradigms that led you to where you are. But if you are in a relationship with someone who threatens violence or follows through on violent threats (whether violence against you or against a wall or even a pillow), please get out now.[42]

Of course, these unhealthy games and control dramas

[42.] We don't have the time in this book to go into truly toxic relationships, how and why we get into them, and how we get out of them, but maybe this book can be a start to help you realize if you're trapped in one. If you are, please try to find help. Turn to therapy, friends, family, anyone who can help you see the truth about what your partner is doing to you—or, on the flip side, the ways in which you are emotionally controlling or hurting your partner.

aren't the only ways we can interact. These are just a few negative ways we can steal energy from one another, often without realizing it. In a healthy relationship, whether a marriage or with your friends or family, hopefully these dramas rarely play out, but know that we are all guilty of them sometimes. Even if you're not an Intimidator, you've probably made your partner feel small, or blamed them for something they didn't deserve blame for to make yourself feel better.

Think about the conversations you have with the people in your life. Think about when you might be playing these games and which ones. If someone you love is using one of these control dramas to steal your energy, sit down and explain it to them. If you discover that you have inadvertently been using one of them to build up your own energy, it's okay. Try to catch yourself the next time; tell your partner you recognize it, and tell them you don't want to interact that way. Ask them to politely point it out if you do it again in the future. All you have to do is be aware going forward and be willing to accept the criticism when it comes. The more you recognize these patterns in yourself and your friends, the better chance you have of fixing them.

Whether through healthy or unhealthy means, everyone needs strokes in their lives. We all need love and recognition (or power and control). We all need validation. The key is to graduate from getting these strokes through petty, unconscious manipulations and get them instead from loving, happy, wonderful, adult relationships. Once we stop depending on control, our lives and relationships can open up. Openness and vulnerability are the only paths to love and acceptance and happiness.

A couple of friends of mine started dating a few months ago. They seemed to be head over heels for one another. But they just broke up. Why? Because she isn't a good listener. And because rather than talk to her about this in a positive way, he got annoyed with her over time and started snapping at her whenever she wouldn't listen. She believed that he wanted her to "change her whole personality" as if not listening well is a personality trait she's looking to hang onto. Her cognitive dissonance fought back hard as she didn't want to accept there was something she needed to change. But when she was legitimately upset at the things he said and the way he said them, he dismissed her feelings and accused her of having a "tizzy fit." Then, after he dumped her, he sent her a podcast on how to listen better. Woof.

The moral of this story is that these two people loved each other. They wanted to be together. And if he had come to her honestly, long before he started snapping at her, in a way that she could have been open to, she could have worked on getting better. Or if he could have listened when she said he had been snapping at her, when she asked him to validate her feelings, they could have both grown together as a couple and as individuals. They are both in the wrong here. But she is probably going to continue going through life not listening to people very well, and he is going to continue letting tiny things build up in relationships until he starts acting like a dick, pushing away anyone who isn't perfect. All they had to do was communicate, be willing to accept their own faults (and each other's), and work toward getting better. Le sigh.

Now here is an example of the opposite of that. During the pandemic, my husband and I had the hardest year of our marriage. We never used to fight, and suddenly we were fighting all the time. Not only that, we were fighting about stupid shit. We were fighting about *how* we were fighting, which is the stupidest shit of all. I have a terrible habit of speaking in superlatives: *you always do this; you always react this way*. And he hated that. He refused to ever admit he was wrong. Ever. Even if he was super-duper 100 percent objectively incorrect. He would just let the fight die, and I would wait for him to apologize and say he was wrong, and it would never come. Those were the heaviest silences of our marriage.

This was the first time in our eight years of marriage that the thought of divorce crossed my mind. Not that I wanted one, but that I knew if this is what our marriage was going to be like, I didn't want the rest of my life to be that way. So we did something really fucking radical: we talked about it.

I came from a house where screaming was a normal Tuesday night. He came from a house where swallowing your feelings is an Olympic sport. Screaming was never an option for him, and every time I raised my voice, he saw our relationship as a toxic failure. He would shut down and end the conversation because nothing can come from screaming. I grew up with a paradigm of yelling is normal, but you always say you're sorry. Neither one of us is right. But we fixed those problems by listening to one another and working hard to stop doing the things we were doing that were hurting the other person. It wasn't easy. I worked hard to stop speaking in superlatives. I worked hard to control the anger that had defined so much of my youth and had sprung up again in the stresses of lockdowns and race riots and moving internationally and being functionally homeless and largely unemployed during a global fucking pandemic. He worked hard to admit that he couldn't admit he was wrong. He says it was the first paradigm shift he has had in a long time. It was hard. Fucking. Work.

I'm not saying I have the secret to a healthy marriage, other than maybe I do. House Rule #2: communicate or die. Tell each other how you're feeling and why you're feeling that way. Listen when someone tells you the way something you said is making them feel, even if you didn't intend it that way. Remember that how someone interpreted what you said holds more weight in their minds than how you meant it. The same is true of friendships and your relationship with your mom and sisters and brothers. We all get stuck in paradigms of action and reaction. Long after I stopped using the superlatives, my husband still assumed I was about to. He thought he knew what I was going to say before I said it, and we are all guilty of that with people we've known for so many years.

Look at all the relationships in your life. Look critically at the dynamics you operate on because every relationship you have has its own. And it won't always be the same every day of the week, but the paradigms are there. If you have unhealthy patterns pre-built into your reactions to certain people or certain situations, it's up to you (and them) to unbuild them and replace them with something better.

Despite getting my temper under control with basically everyone in my life in my early twenties, my family can still trigger me in a moment. My sister is the only one who can have me screaming and losing my shit with just a comment. With any other person, I would be able to separate the toxic, manipulative things she's saying and respond to them in a healthy, grown-up manner (I hope). But it's so hard to unlearn decades of the same dynamic. I'm still working on it.

You have to recognize what kind of comments lead you to react in negative ways. You have to recognize what's happening in your body and create a system for you to respond in a different way than you normally do.

On the other, much brighter side, when relationships are healthy, we don't steal energy from one another; we share it! When a friend is telling me about her job or her kids or whatever else, and I am listening intently, providing support, I am sending her my positive energy and giving her all the strokes she needs (lolz, that sounds dirty, right?). And when she feels that energy, she is unknowingly sending more positive energy right back, and it's a whole, glorious, emotional bucket-filling, happy love fest of a virtuous circle.

Check your life for which of your friends leave you feeling emotionally fulfilled after you hang out and how many make you feel emotionally drained. No, every conversation you have isn't going to be a virtuous cycle. Sometimes you'll just chat about the weather. Sometimes you'll complain, and sometimes you just need a friend to listen. It doesn't make you a "poor me." In all the relationship dynamics we play out, there are plenty of healthy parent-child interactions out there. But how often are you giving and receiving? How often are you the one complaining to your friends, and how often do you let them vent to you? And when they do need to vent, are you really listening, or just waiting for your turn to chime in? When someone tells you a story where something bad happens to them do you immediately respond with a story where something slightly worse happened to you? If so, you may be a one-upper, or playing a game of "Ain't It Awful."

Learn to just listen. Learn what kind of listening your friends are looking for. Do they want advice or just a shoulder to cry on?

As we work to become translucent, we need to be aware of the large and the small. We need to come to terms with the legitimately fucked up shit like that time you threw your co-worker under the bus for something you did, and the tiny, every day fucked up shit, like when your boyfriend was telling you a story, asking for a stroke (definitely dirty), and you were just sitting on your phone. We need to learn how to apologize when someone accuses us of something rather than getting defensive and denying their feelings. No one is perfect; no one is ever going to be perfect. But what if we watched our actions a little more closely? What if we thought about the kind of people we want our friends and partners to be for us and then became that kind of friend or partner to them? What if that's the big secret to figuring out the hard stuff every day?

I will close this chapter on toxic drama llamas with an emphatic caveat: there will be some people in your life who will always be toxic. And I'm sorry to say, but you have to cut them out completely. Not just Linda, who's kind of annoying, and talks shit behind your back, and isn't *really* your friend, but people who are truly, actively holding you back. People who are incapable of having and maintaining healthy relationships, who use manipulation as their only tool of interaction in the world. People who keep you down to make themselves feel better.

Back when we were talking about faults, I mentioned that one of mine is not forgiving. While I do think it's something I can work on, at times, I don't consider it a fault. There are a few people in this world who have shown me who they are through what I call "character defining moments," and that's as much as I need to know them. For every person in my life who has exhibited this kind of terrible behavior, whether insanely selfish or manipulative or anything else, I have tried to have a talk with them about it. A nice grown-up sit-down where I say things like, "Have you considered that when you do that, you're actually doing this?" I have had exactly three of those talks in my life, and two of those three have ended in *those* people cutting off ties with *me*. Why? Because truly toxic people cannot look in the mirror. They cannot become translucent or possibly face who they are. They will use every defense mechanism they can think of to justify their actions. They will gaslight you until you feel like the crazy person. They will intimidate, interrogate, guilt trip, and retreat—every trick in the book.

Sometimes it can take years before you even realize that you are trapped in a dynamic like this. But if you recognize it, and if the person comes back at you with attacks instead of earnest calls for help or a willingness to change (beware the empty promises of "I'm going to get better"), then you need to make some distance. Permanent distance. House Rule #3: don't let the devil inside. I know it can be especially hard with family members, but setting boundaries is critical to your own mental health and growth.

Once you start surrounding yourself with emotionally healthy people, you can look back on where you were before and see how terrible they were so clearly. The guy who made you feel like shit, who threatened to break up with you every other day; it's better to be alone than with him. The friend who constantly puts you down in front of other people and acts like they're just "laughing with you." They're not. That is not how friends treat one another. If you are constantly having to make excuses for a friend or significant other's behavior, ask yourself, *Why? What positive energy are they bringing into my life? Is this relationship worth the energy I am putting into it?*

I hope you're lucky enough that you don't have any people like that in your life. I hope that the people I've had to walk away from in life find their way one day. If any of them ever came to me in earnest, I would 100 percent give them another chance. But if I saw one more hint of toxicity, I'd be gone in a heartbeat. Because I know what healthy relationships look like, and I don't have a minute of this wonderful wacky life on this crazy planet to waste on anything less.

how fast are your windshield wipers wiping?

Man, that was heavy. You probably didn't have time to cut off ties with every toxic person in your life since you just finished reading that last sentence. But maybe you at least have an idea of where to start looking. Hopefully you didn't just discover that you're actually a terrible human being. But even if you did, it's okay. We all have to start somewhere. If you're even willing to admit you may have been a terrible person in the past rather than closing this book, throwing it at the wall, and going to find someone who'll confirm your beliefs that you're a great person, then that's already a huge step in the right direction. Maybe thinking about that last section made you really fucking sad. I get that. Coming to terms with shit is really not a pleasant process. That's probably why we don't do it all that often.

Now that we've talked about coming to terms with how we interact with other people, we need to talk a bit about how we interact with ourselves—how we can become prisoners of our own thoughts. You may be wondering why I keep bringing up windshield wipers. Well, a few years ago, there was a post on Reddit by a person who said they had irrational anxiety that other drivers on the road were judging how fast or slow their windshield wipers were going in the rain. When I first read this, I immediately dismissed it as ludicrous. And then, in the comments, numerous people revealed that they were, in fact, judging other cars on the road for having their wipers at the wrong speed! How absolutely asinine is that?

While this may sound like a counterintuitive argument in a

discussion on irrational anxiety, the ultimate point is that some people are *always* going to judge you for the choices you make. No matter how rich or successful or well-dressed or happily married or no matter how abso-fucking-lutely perfect your life is—and no matter if your windshield wipers are always at the ideal wiping interval—someone is still going to judge you. And you can continue to let that bother you, or you can not. Those are the only two choices.

Changing the way you look, changing your job, and changing the way you define success to better align with your authentic ideal are all great steps on the path to happiness and contentment. Changing the way you react to negative events in your life is critical to your own sense of accomplishment and your ability to survive and overcome adversity. Losing bad habits and giving up meaningless shopping or drinking or whatever to fill the voids in your life is a necessary step towards creating a meaningful and fulfilled existence. But ultimately, you have to make real changes on the inside before any of those things will stick. If you give up your bad habits on the outside, but make no real changes to the way you see and interact with the world, before long they will creep right back in. You can move to Paris, but if you don't address the root of what's been making you unhappy, Paris will still suck. At some point, you just have to stop giving a shit about your windshield wipers.

I have a friend. Let's call her Laura. She is an emotional basket-case. She bounces from one end of her brain to the other like a monkey on a pogo stick in a room made of trampolines. She imagines insane and unlikely scenarios where her boyfriend suddenly doesn't like her or never did. She reads into his every move, analyzing and searching and picking in hopes that she can discover proof of how he doesn't love her anymore. For the record, he does love her, and they are very happy. But for her, even though she knows these thoughts are crazy, she can't stop them from coming. She knows these emotions make her sound like an insane person, so she doesn't share them. In not sharing them, she harbors them, and they fester. As they fester, she becomes less trusting and more suspect of his every move. Her distance becomes palpable and leads to him drawing away, which only proves her original suspicion correct that he never loved her in the first place!

Obviously, that's wrong. This is a self-fulfilling prophecy. It came true, but only because she made it so. It's so easy to get caught in this endless loop of feeling worry and anxiety and then feeling anxious about it so you worry more. You know that you shouldn't feel that way and you shouldn't be thinking these things and then you beat yourself up for not being so normal. Why can't you just have normal thoughts like everyone else?

I won't lie and say everyone suffers from this kind of anxiety; I don't. I have my own special brand that I'll talk about later. But the point is to know that plenty of people do. And it's okay. So long as you are able to recognize when it's happening. As long as you can identify these feelings for what they are, you can manage your reaction to them. Is it ridiculous to feel anxiety about whether or not people are judging you for how fast your windshield wipers are wiping? Of course it is, and surely the people who feel that anxiety are already aware of this. I have a very confident and well-adjusted friend who gets worried the cashier at the supermarket is judging him whenever he buys toilet paper. As if they are staring at the twenty-four-roll jumbo pack thinking, "This freak WIPES."

But when those feelings of anxiety and worry start creeping into your brain, you have to have the presence of mind to recognize them and to name them in order to control them. The same way we have to recognize patterns of behavior with other people, we have to work to recognize these patterns with ourselves. Overcoming anxiety doesn't mean not having anxious thoughts; it means not letting them control you when they come.

I have a tendency to get irrational sometimes. Sometimes when I'm PMSing, other times when I can't seem to explain it at all, I will feel extreme feelings. It doesn't happen often, but it happens. I will be overwhelmed with sadness; I will be overcome with anger. I will cry in the middle of the day or snap at my husband when he doesn't deserve it. I will argue illogical points for no discernible reason. I also have irrational anxiety about trips that I've taken, that I picked the wrong city or the wrong hotel. I have what is known as FOBO (fear of better options). I worry that the people I'm traveling with aren't having a great time, and because I am always the one to plan trips, it's all on me. And this anxiety has stayed with me for *years* after I get back from a trip. Years. It will pop into my head like, *Goddamnit why didn't we stay at Troux-aux Biches instead of Flic-en-Flac?!* How completely absurd is that? But you know what I did when it started getting really bad? I recognized it. I worked on it. I talked to my husband about it and tried to identify it when it was coming. I made a point to compartmentalize those thoughts as ridiculous. I felt so much guilt for not planning the perfect trip that I basically ruined a vacation to a tropical fucking island. Not cool, Taylor.

    I cannot always control these emotions. I can't stop them from coming, and I can't always make them go away once they come. But what I can do is label them for what they are. I can tell my husband: "I am sorry I am being very irrational; I appreciate your patience while we await my return to normalcy." I remind myself again and again, *thoughts are not facts.* And that's the best we can do. The best we can do is to look at ourselves honestly and try to see our behavior from the other side and to tell the people in our lives who might be affected by it. And honestly, it's gotten better over the years. I don't have the same mood swings or snap at my husband for no reason (at least not very often). I don't get so hung up on planning a less-than-perfect trip because perfect is the enemy of great. Who knew we could actually grow as humans!

    When Laura has those thoughts about her boyfriend, she knows she is being irrational. She knows her fears are unfounded and that venturing further down that rabbit hole will only lead to heartache. She knows it will only further alienate herself from him to listen to those thoughts. So she started being honest with her boyfriend. When she starts to feel that panic creeping up in her chest, she tells him. It's still hard for him to deal with it sometimes, but that's okay. That's part of her, and she's trying to get better, and she's doing the best she can.

I originally wrote that story about Laura when I started writing this book back in 2017. I am happy to report that after a lot of work, she realized this anxiety trap was created from her ex-boyfriend who was constantly threatening to leave her, gaslighting her, and making her feel like a crazy person. He accused her of cheating every time she left the house. He would stop talking to her for days at a time. He was emotionally and verbally abusive for many years. The worst part is, she didn't even know she was being verbally abused for years until a conversation with her dad helped her see what was happening and that she wasn't crazy—her ex did this *to* her. And she could have remained in those anxiety patterns for the rest of her life. But she didn't. Luckily, she found a wonderful man who was willing to work through it with her, who was willing to be patient when she needed it and assuage her anxieties when they started to take over. She recognized them and talked about them and found a healthy person to help her regain her confidence in herself. Hooray! They are happily married now, by the way, and just had their first baby.

I am not a psychologist (obviously), and this isn't a book focused on diagnosing and curing anxiety disorders. If this is something you seriously struggle with, there are a ton of other, more helpful books out there on the topic. But even if you don't have a diagnosed anxiety disorder (I do not), there are still plenty of us who overthink things sometimes or fall into patterns of negative thinking that can stress us out unnecessarily.

We doubt ourselves, wondering if we are good parents or good partners or if that email we sent at work was embarrassing. We wonder if the work we do is good enough, if anything we do is good enough. We read into comments from our bosses that we definitely bombed that last presentation. We compare ourselves to others around us because everyone else is definitely perfect and I am the only crazy, shitty person here, obviously. And even when people we love tell us, "You're being ridiculous, I think you're reading too much into this" we dismiss it. We tell them they couldn't possibly know.

Back on my list of my biggest faults you might remember reading "overly critical of myself." Welp, I don't worry how fast my windshield wipers are wiping, I just worry that I am an utter and complete failure, that every dinner I make is trash, and that pretty much nothing I do is worth a dime. I put too much on myself, then feel guilty for not doing enough, and then start apologizing to my husband for not doing enough who then has to reassure me that everything is fine even though nothing was fucking wrong in the first place. Which game is this? Oh yeah, "There I Go Again" (poor me, self-deprecating, looking for reassurance). Damn, that book had me pegged. And my husband has the patience of a saint.

In that spirit, I would like to provide a quick guide to avoid some common traps of negative thinking. Even if you don't have an anxiety disorder, these tools can be used to readjust your perspective when bad things happen (or when you imagine them happening) and reset the narrative playing in your head.

If you ever get caught in one of these anxiety traps where you feel like you're spiraling out, the first little mantra you can turn to is the one I like to use: *thoughts are not facts*. Whatever type of self-doubt or anxiety trap you find yourself caught in, that statement remains an actual, real, fact. No matter how real and legitimate the thoughts in your brain feel, it doesn't make them reality. What evidence do you have to believe this thought is true?

The next thing you need to do is identify which kind of thinking you might be engaging in. One of the most common anxiety traps is catastrophizing, where you can only imagine the worst-case scenario, no matter how unlikely that is. I promise, you are not going to get fired because your presentation wasn't perfect. Your boyfriend isn't going to dump you because you burned the casserole. And if he is, then good riddance.

Another is all-or-nothing thinking that leads you to create two black-and-white extremes of potential outcomes while ignoring the much more likely outcome of "somewhere in the middle." Most things in life are grey. Just because you have a fight with your friend doesn't mean you're a stupid loser and everyone hates you. You had one fight with one friend, and she doesn't even hate you. It's okay.

Fortunetelling is when you think you can predict the future, but you obviously cannot. You have no idea whether your presentation is going to be a disaster or whether no one at the party is going to talk to you, so just stop. Repeat after me: *thoughts are not facts.*

Mind-reading is probably the most common trap, believing that you know what other people are thinking, and that it's definitely negative. You don't know what other people are thinking, and it isn't definitely negative. Here's the real kicker—most people don't even think that much about other people at all! Everyone's too busy worrying about themselves. And even if people are thinking negative things about you, just remember all that other stuff we talked about—about not caring because it doesn't matter anyway. Anyone thinking pointlessly negative things about you isn't worth your time in the first place. Your windshield wipers are perfectly fine.

These are just a few examples of the ways we let our thoughts control us, but there are many others. Your own anxiety may be very serious, or it may be mild, or you may not suffer from it at all (congratulations!), but most of us have gone down these anxiety traps about one thing or another. If you find yourself spiraling out, you need to recognize the thinking pattern that you're dealing with. Maybe you default to one of these, or maybe a mix of a few, or maybe you have your very own special pattern that you invented like Laura did. Either way, you need to get better about recognizing when it's coming. Maybe there are physical symptoms that precede it like increased heartrate, or you start picking at something or biting your nails. As neuroscientist Judson Brewer suggests, get curious about the sensations that come along with your anxiety. Awareness is an incredibly powerful tool. Once you can recognize your pattern, name it. Know what you call it when it's happening so you can make it "an other." Such as, "Oh shit, I got the willy wonks starting again!" Make it a thing that is separate from who you are and your real, valid thoughts.

Cognitive Behavior Therapy, or CBT, was developed in the 1960s as a way to treat clinical depression. Over the years, it's been proven to work as a method against all kinds of issues from social anxiety to eating disorders and obsessive-compulsive tendencies.[43] The main concept is that while there are a million things in the world around you cannot control (the things that cause your anxiety), you *can* control how you think about them. Once again, I'm not a licensed professional—and I highly recommend you see one if your anxiety is debilitating—but many of the approaches are things you can start working on in your daily life. CBT can help you deal with all of the different cognitive distortions you may suffer from, whether overgeneralization or all-or-nothing thinking. It helps you to see those thinking patterns as they arise and put them where they belong.

One of the first things you can do at home is to start journaling when these thoughts come up. You can include the time of the mood, the source of it, the intensity, everything. The more you journal each time you have a reaction, the easier it is to see it coming. You can also ask yourself pointed questions about why you're thinking a certain thing will happen. Ask yourself if you could be misinterpreting evidence. Ask yourself if you are taking all the evidence into account, or just the pieces that support your view that you're a failure or you're definitely going to get fired.

[43.] You can find some more detailed guides and worksheets at this website: https://positivepsychology.com/cbt-cognitive-behavioral-therapy-techniques-worksheets/

Ask yourself if a friend came to you with this same problem, what would you say to them? Would you tell them their life is over, or would you tell them to look at the evidence and realize it probably isn't as bad as they think?

    I like to play the worst-case-scenario game. Play out several different options of the situation that is stressing you out. Maybe the best-case scenario is your friend isn't even mad about what you said, and everything is fine. The middle-of-the-road scenario is that she is pissed, but you can talk to her and apologize, and it will be alright. And the worst-case scenario is that she is so angry she never wants to speak to you again. Okay, well that sucks, but it doesn't mean your life is over. It means you had a shitty friend who lacks conflict resolution skills. The idea is to get to the worst-case scenario and realize that no matter what it is, it's something you can handle. Because you can handle anything. Everyone can. You have survived everything that has happened to you so far.

    My FOBO thinking was irrational, and it probably took me about a year to recognize it, make it an other, and stop it from infecting my own happiness like a virus. The worst part was that it took my husband even longer to see that I had changed. He assumed I was still being negative and seeing the worst in things. He thought I was having a terrible time on a trip because I said we should have rented a car instead of taking the bus (we totes should have), but it wasn't ruining the trip. I was having the time of my life in the motherfucking Seychelles looking at the most beautiful electric blue water I had seen in my entire life! And yet, because of the patterns I had set out, he had no way of knowing that. He only heard me complain about that bus and thought I was spiraling out in the same ways I had before.

    It is up to us to not only work towards being better, to work towards fixing the parts of ourselves we don't like, but also to understand it can take time for others to recognize those changes in us. We have to be ready to be patient, and to help those we love see our growth. This probably all sounds pretty hard and shitty, huh? It sounds like even when you do the hard work and

how fast are your windshield wipers wiping? | 197

make real progress, you can still be met with fights and frustrations and like what's even the point?! Which leads me to my next, all-important piece of advice.

communicate or die

When you have feelings, no matter how crazy: share them with someone. Hiding your emotions on any subject, on any topic, is unhealthy. If you don't feel like you have someone to share with, go on Reddit. Seriously. Reddit is full of people who share some of their deepest, darkest insecurities and worries and phobias and idiosyncrasies. If you can't tell a friend, tell a stranger. Tell me. When we keep our emotions and our fears locked inside, it affects us. They fester. Honest human connection is literally the answer to trauma, the answer to growth, the answer to healing, and the answer to happiness. You may be surprised to learn how many other people are going through the exact same thing as you.

I want you to think for a moment about the people in your life. Who is your best friend? Who do you trust? Is there anyone who knows everything about you? There is a scene in the 1998 movie *Meet Joe Black* (an underrated classic if you ask me) where Joe, who is death personified trying to understand human love, asks Jeffrey Tambor how he knows his wife loves him. And Tambor replies, "Because she knows the worst thing about me, and it's okay."

That has always stuck with me. Because somewhere along the line—either because of or despite being raised in a family with a lying, narcissistic father and a couple compulsively-lying siblings—I decided that honesty was the most important thing. Honesty with yourself and others. I don't want to be in a relationship or a friendship if it means I have to hide part of myself, and neither should you. There is no more liberating feeling than knowing that a person knows the worst thing about you, and it's okay. And it isn't just about romantic love. Every human on this planet needs a person. A person to confide in; a person who will hold your secrets and share the weight of them; a person you know will accept whatever you tell them—even if they judge you a little at first, it's still okay. I can't tell you I know how to find this person if you don't already have one. I can tell you that showing up to life with honesty and being vulnerable to other people can open up relationships in the least likely places. We have all trained ourselves to be reserved because it's socially appropriate. When people ask us how we are, they don't mean it, and we don't tell them. But maybe, just once, try to put yourself out there. Confide in another parent at the soccer game that you're having a hard day. Reach out to an old friend you've lost touch with and tell them you miss them.

Psychologist and self-help guru Brené Brown talks about the three core principles of wholehearted living: love, belonging, and vulnerability. Vulnerability is at the core of all human interaction, and yet we have worked so hard to program it out of ourselves. We yearn to be strong, tough, and unflappable. We stop opening ourselves up to others because it means we can potentially get hurt. But that's the rub: there is no love without vulnerability. There is no belonging without love. And without love, we wither. In Brown's research at the University of Houston, she discovered that the people who had a strong sense of love and belonging believed they deserved it and were worthy of it. Believing you deserve connectedness leads to greater connection. When old people lack human connection, they literally fucking die.[44]

Maybe you got burned in a bad relationship and decided you wouldn't put yourself out there again. Maybe you opened

---

[44] Kassandra Alcaraz, et al., "Social Isolation and Mortality in US Black and White Men and Women," *American Journal of Epidemiology*, Volume 188, Issue 1 (January 2019): 102–109, https://doi.org/10.1093/aje/kwy231.

up to a friend about your anxiety, and they laughed at you, and you've never talked about it since. Whatever traumas in your life—whether macro or micro—led you to close off certain parts of yourself, just know you are not alone. Not by a long shot. I think there has been a reckoning about this in the last few years as well: we're all fucked up. Everyone. Anyone who isn't processing some part of their past is either lying or in denial. And I think the conversations we're able to have about mental health these days are so fucking healthy. It's absolutely miraculous. I swear, thirty-something women in 2022 are just owning their own mental health and sharing everything all over the place. "Hey girl, wanna come over and process some traumas?" We're being honest and vulnerable and putting ourselves out there because it's the only way to heal, and it's the only way to cultivate the healthy relationships we need to be happy in this life.

As much as sharing our own hurts and truths is important, communicate or die goes the other way as well. We have to tell people when the way they're treating us is wrong or hurtful or fucked up. Tell Linda that shit is not fucking cool. Stop apologizing for other people or sugarcoating everything and walking on eggshells. If you can't be honest with someone, they aren't your real friend. Even if it's hard for them to hear, even if they lash out at you and tell you you're being a real dick—it's not being a dick to set boundaries with the people in your life. If no one tells us when we fuck up, it's really hard for us to see it in ourselves. Maybe Linda will be pissed off for a while, but maybe, hopefully, she'll realize that what you're saying is coming from the right place. It's coming from a place of wanting to help, but also needing your own feelings to be heard and validated. Demand the best from the people in your life and give them the best in return.

When I got the idea for this book, I started writing a confident diatribe about eschewing all things mainstream and owning whoever you are no matter the consequences. And I believe in that. At least in the latter part most fervently. But in the spirit of radical honesty, I also thought it important to remind you, and to remind myself, that no matter how far I've come from seventh grade, no matter how brazenly I disregard the opinions of others, they still matter to me. They can't not.

This part is harder to write than I thought it would be. I almost typed the words, then didn't. Then I wrote these introductory sentences instead to delay just one more moment. But here we go. My biggest fear isn't something that keeps me awake at night. It isn't even something I realized about myself until quite recently. And beginning to write this book is what brought about the realization in the first place.

My biggest fear is being ostracized. Not by some particular person or some girl who holds a grudge against me, but by everyone. By my closest friends. My biggest fear is not of being alone. I know how to be alone. I can always meet new people once I'm alone. But a dark and quiet part of myself never wants anyone to push me out. The jeers and sneers and whispers behind my back scare me more than dying an old lady with no offspring to care for me. I'm no psychologist, but it's pretty clear that's rooted in the most traumatic memories of my youth—in the kids who made me feel so alone in the first place, and so much like I couldn't be myself. But that's neither here nor there.

I say fuck the mainstream, fuck the rules, fuck what I'm supposed to do. But at the end of the day, I still hope someone likes me for that. I still hope my brash, abrasive nature is interpreted as charming and my scathing sarcasm is interpreted as wit.

I hope people like me. And that's okay. It's okay to feel that way; it's okay to want that. So long as the actions you're taking are true to yourself, then somebody will. Not everybody. But I learned a long time ago that you don't need everybody to like you. Most people suck anyway. You just need one or two good ones to recognize and reciprocate the beautiful, wonderful, authentically weird person inside of yourself.

the happiness conundrum

While we're on the topic of radical honesty, I recently saw an old friend from high school whom I hadn't seen in eleven years. He came to pick me up to grab a drink, and when I asked, "How's your COVID year been?" moments after seeing him for the first time in a decade, he unloaded everything on me. Losing two jobs and two girlfriends, moving back in with his parents at thirty-eight, feeling utterly lost and hopeless, like a complete fucking failure. His year was, without a doubt, way worse than the hard one I had. But the beauty of it struck me: that there has been no shame in struggling the past two years. If anything, it's weirder if you weren't struggling. Whether you lost your job and were trying to redefine yourself during unemployment, whether you started working from home and had to deal with never-ending Zoom meetings and virtual learning for your three kids, whether you were working in a hospital or working at a grocery store or just fucking existing the last two years—it's been hard.

There is a lot of talk about toxic positivity going around right now. For the past decade we've all been hearing that we need to find happiness, and be positive, and it's totally up to us—and all those things are true. But acting like it's possible to be happy all the time is toxic and damaging. The deeper truth is that we need to embrace the hardest parts. 2020 was hard for almost everyone. So was 2021. And it was almost as if this collective struggle finally allowed us to collectively open up about how much we've been struggling. And maybe now that we can all agree that life is hard for everyone sometimes, we can stop pretending like there are people who are always happy. We can stop pretending like celebrities and Instagram influencers have perfect lives, and we can stop trying to shove any feelings of unhappiness deep into our gullets whenever they start bubbling up at the surface. There is no joy without pain, and allowing that pain to exist is a very real part of being happy in the end.

We want to be happy. As much as possible, all the time, every day. And whether that happiness comes from a healthy, loving, supportive relationship with your bestie or six hours of TV and a bottle of wine that temporarily numb all the terrible shit in your life . . . the reality is that neither thing is ever really going to work. Calm down, I don't mean it like that. Of course you can be happy in a lot of your life. But there is no person who is happy all the time. There is no person who doesn't experience mood swings or bouts of uncertainty. The worst part is that even knowing that everyone else on the planet experiences these things doesn't make it feel any better or any less real. It doesn't make me feel any less sad in this very moment even though I have no idea why I'm feeling sad, I just kinda woke up this way.

The point is that's okay. And maybe your swings of happiness are broader than others. Maybe sometimes you're down for longer than others. That's okay too. As long as you're honest with yourself and the people around you. Tell your husband that you're feeling sad today and hope that it gets better tomorrow. Tell yourself you're feeling sad today, and that's okay, and hope that it gets better tomorrow. Life is about cycles and balance and yin and yang and there is no winter without summer and no joy without sorrow. Let's stop pretending it's possible—or even desirable—to be happy all the time.

Think about the last time you were sad or depressed or upset. Did you try to hide it? Did you put on a pretty face and go to work and go through your day and just kind of pretend everything was okay? When someone asked, how are you? Did you say, "I'm fine," and then proceed to definitely not tell them at all how you were feeling inside? Did you confide in a friend or tell your significant other? We are so conditioned to believe that there is something wrong with being sad that we are ashamed of it. We think it's something to hide while we put only our best face forward. We cry in the bathroom at work, and then wipe off our tears, fix our makeup, and go back to our desks. What, you never cried in the bathroom at work before? Lucky you.

If you're a man, this is probably a hundred times worse, and you don't even realize it. Men are so conditioned not to express emotion that they literally go their whole lives being told that "real men don't cry," and then they just bottle up all their feelings until eventually they punch someone? This is my entire understanding of masculinity. Please correct me if I'm wrong.

But what if it was okay to just *be* sad? What if instead of trying to do some happiness exercises or writing in your gratitude journal or posting a feel-good quote on Instagram, you just let it happen? What if when someone asked how you are, it was normal to respond, "I'm just a little sad today, I'm not sure why." Or maybe you do know why, and you could answer without feeling like you were unfairly burdening your friend or coworker or whomever. If you experience a loss in your life (whether a job or a pet or a loved one), you don't have to be happy. If someone tells you to "just to stay positive" tell them to just go fuck themselves because it's literally toxic. They are denying the reality and validity of your emotions, even though it is often well-intentioned. And whether you realize it or not, they are making you feel shame for having those emotions. This mentality makes everyone feel like it's weird to be unhappy. That when something bad happens you just dust yourself off and pull yourself up by those magical bootstraps![45]

When I get sad, I like to think about Eeyore. Eeyore was basically suffering from clinical depression every single day of his life. Pooh and Tigger didn't tell him to just smile, or get over

---

[45]. Fun fact: the phrase "pull yourself up by your bootstraps" was originally meant as a sarcastic, impossible paradox. Because you obviously cannot pull yourself up by your own boot. And now we unironically tell people to do it all the time. Please stop saying this.

it, or any other platitude you can think of—they just loved their friend. I have a friend who is somewhat manic depressive. She goes through huge swings when she is up and active and driven and excited about the world . . . and then I won't hear from her for weeks or months as she shuts down and beats herself up and loses all motivation to do anything. Whenever I see her falling back into a depressive state, I just let her know I'm there for her. That's it. I don't expect anything from her other than being my friend whenever she's ready to come back. I know if she wants to talk to me at any time that she knows I'll be there for her. Because I always have been. Because I've never made her feel shitty for disappearing for a month or two (though it took some time for me to understand that her disappearing had nothing to do with me).

How about this: the next time you feel sad or lonely or unhappy or whatever, put on some extra sad music or watch a really sad movie and just *own* it. Feel all the feelings; don't deny them. Find people in your life who accept you when you're sad the same as when you're happy. Find people in your life who encourage you to do that. Find the person who will come over with some ice cream and two bottles of wine and watch ugly-cry-face movies with you and not expect anything more or spend two hours trying to cheer you up. Maybe I don't just have a "case of the Mondays," Linda.

Finding your authentic self, listening to your heart, following your dreams, not giving a fuck—whatever you want to call it—won't make you happy every day. Because nothing will make you happy every day. Because no one is happy every day. It's just part of our existence. Life is still hard sometimes, even when you're doing exactly what you love and living by your own rules. But as soon as you're not expecting to be bouncing over rainbows, you'll be okay with being sad from time to time. And in some strange way, accepting that sadness actually makes you happier. It's the Backwards Law.

at the end of the day

At this point we've covered a lot of the most common problems we suffer from on the inside. We refuse to recognize our own faults while always seeing them (and pointing them out) in other people. We stay in toxic relationships (or perpetuate them) because we're not used to seeing what truly healthy ones look like. We beat ourselves up because we're not happy all the time, even though there is no such thing. We spiral out into negative thought patterns telling ourselves we aren't good enough, or we're going to fail, or we should have been better even though the only people those hurt is you and those closest to you.

But once we get past our most negative and toxic behaviors, what happens next? Who is your ideal self on a daily basis? Obviously, we won't all have the same ideal; we all wrote different lists at the beginning of this book about being funny or charming or witty or dependable or intelligent, and that's wonderful. Whatever things you wrote on that list, you should absolutely strive to be. But at the core of it, there are some things that every human should be, that every human should share. There are ideals that are universal on this crazy, hurtling pinpoint in space.

What if, aside from your own unique characteristics that make you exactly who you are, your ideal self wasn't to be a doctor or to make a million dollars, but was to just be the best person you could be to other people? And every time you made a decision, it was guided by that concept: is this how I would want to be treated? What if that golden rule we all grew up being taught, whether in church or at home or in school, was actually the secret to happiness all along? What if the only thing you really had to do was *unto others as you would have them do unto you?*

I know, crazy, right!? It's SO SIMPLE. Treat other people the way you want to be treated. Don't be a dick. Prepare to have your mind blown here: what if we all strive to become *good*? Good friends, good mothers, good fathers, good husbands and wives, good sons and daughters. Good people to strangers. Does my husband need a little extra patience tonight because he had a hard day? Maybe I should call my best friend I haven't talked to in months. And what about for strangers? Did I need to cut that guy off in traffic to get to where I was going fifteen seconds sooner? If the tables were turned, how would that have made me feel?

Maybe when we look at our tree-clouds, we don't pay attention to which college we went to or which career path we took. Maybe we stop lingering on the relationship we fucked up or the embarrassing shit we did. Maybe the only decisions that really matter are the tiny ones. Maybe this whole idea of success and our lives and our paths and having a kind of direction was all a lie? Maybe literally the only thing that matters is how we treat other people? Maybe the tree-cloud was never a tree at all.

Back when my husband and I lived in Cape Town, I was driving him to work one morning, and we had to merge into a very difficult-to-merge place. I didn't usually drive him during rush hour, and everyone was angry and selfish and didn't want to let other drivers in. Immediately I joined in the frustration. As I was bitching about how I was never gonna get in, trying to inch the front of our tiny car farther out into the intersection, my husband turned to me and said, "You know, I just decided this was a thing I wasn't gonna get mad about. So I wave people in front of me and smile and then maybe I'm two minutes later to work." And that was it. He just decided not to be negative, to not get mad when someone didn't let him in, and to return that rudeness with kindness for the next person. He decided to be nice to a stranger, and everyone's day was better for it. Including his own. What a fucking saint I married.

Try it sometime. Think about someone other than yourself. Separate yourself from all the things that weigh you down every single day, the things that happen to us that are so easy to get lost in, and suddenly weeks and years have gone by on autopilot. You write your to-do lists, you go to work, you go to the grocery store, you get pissed at the guy in traffic, and you forget to actually enjoy the life you inhabit. It's about living with intention rather than floating through endless repetitive days forgetting to remember what makes life worth living: the people we love. One day, if you're lucky enough to grow old, you're gonna wake up and eighty years of your life will be gone, and you'll have no fucking idea where it went. Hopefully you will have had someone to love.

A couple years ago at a New Year's Eve party, just before my thirty-fifth birthday would ring in at midnight, my friends and I solved the meaning of life. Or, at the very least, we discovered the only two things every person needs to be happy: gratitude and validation. We spent the rest of the night toasting to gratitude and validation again and again, everyone telling everyone how wonderful they are and all the wonderful things they bring into our lives. You need to have gratitude for everything that you have. You need to accept those negative experiences in order to turn them into positive experiences. It may sound cheesy to have a gratitude journal, but it works. Because it's easy to forget how many things we have. Because the hedonic treadmill is constantly resetting our status quos.

Finding happiness in this world isn't about searching for it or achieving something. It's about already being happy with what you have. And when you are a person who is truly happy with who you are and what you have—a person who is honest with themselves and others—you no longer have to go searching for something. You won't find yourself complaining and putting out so much negative energy into the world that you will just get right back; you'll find yourself surrounded by positivity. You'll find yourself creating that positivity in others. It truly is infectious!

The other half of this equation is validation. When you have gratitude for the wonderful people in your life, you tell them, and they receive the validation they need to feel happy and safe. Belonging and esteem are biological human needs. We don't just want to feel loved and appreciated, we physically need it. And the way to manifest that validation is to put positivity out into the world. It's a virtuous circle: the happier you are with your life, the more you appreciate people and tell them why they are wonderful, the more they receive your validation and send gratitude right back to you for being who you are, and then you get the validation you need in return. It's one big love fest, and it's a wonderful fucking way to be.

Now think about the opposite. Think about that friend of yours who always complains about everything. No matter what thing you say to cheer them up or offer a solution to their problem, they just dismiss it. They are inconsolable. The world sucks, everything sucks, and life is unfair. Eventually, the negative energy they bring into the world seeps into your world view. They never seem to thank you for being a friend, and you feel frustrated, angry, and drained. You want to be a good friend to this person, but it's just getting so hard. I don't know if you can help this friend or not. But I think you need to be honest with that friend about their negativity. Tell them what you need in a friend. Tell them you want to be there for them, but you can't help them if they don't want to be helped.

I want you to think about every single person in your life. This should be easy since you already did it when we Marie Kondo'd our friend list. For every person who is in your life, think about your relationship with them. Hopefully you already got rid of the obviously toxic people—the ones like Laura's ex-boyfriend or the ones using control dramas to drain your energy. Or hopefully, if you were that person, you figured out how to break that cycle and start forging healthier relationships.

It's possible at this point, if you've really been working on making changes, that you don't have that many friends remaining. And that's okay. Because it just means you are making room for the better, stronger relationships you're going to be building the rest of your life. But back to the people who are left: the friends whom you have always been able to be yourself around: your supportive spouse, your sister, whoever. For each of those people, write a list of reasons why you value them, why they stayed in your life. Fuck it, while you're at it, just write a letter.

Now is the time to be grateful for the people in your life who have been there, who have accepted you, who have let you be both happy and sad. Even if the only person on that list is your mom, it's okay. Write down the list or write a letter with all the reasons why they are still in your life. And then tell them. Send them the letter. Sit down and have a drink with them and tell them everything. Be vulnerable. Show gratitude. Give them the validation they deserve. Maybe it's an older friend you haven't seen in a long time but you want to finally reconnect with. Put yourself out there. You have no idea how much that person could be wanting to hear from you. And if they ignore your calls or tell you they're too busy; that's okay. Maybe they aren't ready yet, and maybe they are still so caught up in their own lives they just can't think about anyone else. The sad reality is that most people don't.

I've been trying to really reconnect with one of my sisters for years. She is always too busy, never has time, and only talks about herself and her kids when we do have the time to talk. She never picks up the phone and rarely responds to my texts. Once every two or three years when I see her in person, she constantly interrupts me, her fluttering brain ever jumping back to her own problems in her own world. She never asks how I am; I don't think she even knows what I do. I highly doubt she'll ever even read this book. It breaks my heart, but she's my sister, and I hope one day she can open herself back up to the love and support I am ready and willing to give. Just know that everyone won't be ready to suddenly have these wonderful, open, honest, authentic, life-changing, soul-validating relationships. But hopefully they will. And if not, hopefully your words will begin to wake them up to what they're missing.

If you don't have anyone meaningful left in your life, or if you didn't really have anyone before you started this book, then you need to ask yourself why. Have you been open and honest with other people? Have you been kind? Or have you maybe been as selfish and self-absorbed as most of us are in our daily lives? It's just too easy to get wrapped up in our own shit that we forget that we have to *make* time for people. If living abroad for so many years has taught me anything, it's that friendships are work. If I don't take the time to schedule video chats or send a text when someone pops into my head, these friendships would whither so quickly across an ocean, across a six- or seven- or thirteen-hour time difference. Friendships are hard to build and easy to lose.

I know it can be hard to make friends, especially later in life, but try an app. I made a friend on Bumble BFF when I moved to Madrid, and she is incredible. She is kind and caring and open and honest and funny, and I think she recognizes those things in me as well. I know it's (yet another) cliché, but join some shit. Bowling, disc golf, knitting—find a group on Facebook or Reddit for whatever it is you're into. No matter what you're into, there is a group on the internet devoted to it. If you are really putting out an honest version of yourself—if you are working to be happy and allowing yourself to be sad and working towards vulnerability and just having an authentic human experience that you're trying to share with another authentic human—there will be someone. And if you can't find anyone, talk to me. Just be prepared to hear some brutal honesty from my end if you do.

It's critical to note in all this that self-care is, well, critical. You absolutely shouldn't sacrifice everything that's important to you for other people. Being a great mom doesn't mean never having alone time. The beauty of this concept is that if everyone were to act this way—to try to give the people we love what they need as much as possible—we wouldn't have to work so hard to scrape together resources for our own self-care. And sorry guys, but this is just so much more true for most women, and especially mothers. If you are a person who gives too much and leaves nothing for yourself, then do exactly the opposite. Ask yourself why you find it necessary to sacrifice your own time to please other people. Ask yourself which things you can say *no* to. And start saying no. The golden rule applies here too—if you are constantly ignoring your own needs, dropping everything whenever your friend needs you no matter what's going on in your own life, would you really want them to do the same? Of course not. You want your friend to be happy and healthy and to take care of themselves as well. If you'd rather your friend had a worse life to make your own life better, well then you have some much more serious issues to work through.

Setting healthy boundaries is healthy for everyone involved. Self-care is part of being truly authentic. It's part of owning yourself and who you are and what you want and what you need, no matter what those things are. We don't have to ignore our own desires and sacrifice in order to be good to people. When you stop living your life for other people, dressing for other people, pleasing other people, trying to be perfect, trying to have it all, you'll be able to see so clearly what it is that you need. Maybe that's quitting your job and traveling the world. Or maybe it's just leaving work a little earlier and having more date nights with your partner.

The truth is that taking care of yourself—giving yourself whatever it is that you need—allows you to take better care of others too. If you're miserable on the inside, you won't be any good to anyone else either. No matter how we get there, we can all agree that the world is a better place when we are more kind, more forgiving, more attentive, and more present.

When your ideal self is to be the kindest, most generous person you can be, your life will be filled with joy. Joy is infectious. When we bring it to others, it makes them happy and makes us happy. In fact, doing things for other people actually increases our happiness more than doing things for ourselves! If you're into the Law of Attraction (I'm way too cynical for that shit, but it can help with overcoming negativity), you'll know that what you put out into the world is what you attract. Positivity attracts positivity, and negativity breeds more negativity. It's about taking a moment to appreciate all the wonderful moments we have each day. Grab your husband's butt while he's doing the dishes. Tell your friend you love her sweater. Fuck it, tell Linda you love her sweater. Spread joy in all the little things you do, and you'll get it right back.

If every day this is your goal, and you start to recognize the real joy that comes from all the smallest things, the bigger car and the bigger house just won't seem to matter as much. Loving, authentic, deep, reciprocal relationships are the only thing worth living for. You wanna cure cancer while you're at it? That's amazing. Just don't be a dick along the way. There is no switch I can pull in your brain to help you see that. You can try going to the Serengeti or moving to New Zealand, but once you learn it, you can never unlearn it. Nothing will ever matter to you more than love and kindness and sharing that love and kindness with others.

Whoever you do end up finding in this crazy life, whether friend, lover, or sibling, be sure to treat them the way you would want to be treated. Give them the kindness and attention that you want to be given by others. Listen when they talk, ask them about that thing at work, let them be sad when they need to be sad. Validate them by telling them how much they mean to you. Be grateful for their presence in your life, and be grateful for all the wonderful things you have. Because, at the end of the day, loving and being loved is really the only thing that matters in this stupid, fucked up world.

epilogue

pale blue dot

Ah shit, did I just make it sound like once you realize love and joy and kindness are all that matters that you will never get sucked into the rat race again? That you will never get caught up in the bullshit that makes us sad and makes us feel worthless—makes us feel *less than*?

Well, I'm sorry for making you think that was possible even just for a second. But didn't the end of that chapter feel so *good?* Unfortunately, knowing and even experiencing this great truth in life won't make you immune to the bullshit. I spent most of 2021 having one of the worst years of my life, despite having moved to an incredible city and making wonderful new friends. Despite getting my happy marriage back after all the issues my husband and I worked through, I still felt like shit. Closing my publishing business left me feeling worthless. I guess all these decades of living in late-stage capitalism were more deeply ingrained than I thought. If I wasn't producing something, where was my worth? I wasn't working in a bar or saving to travel; I was just sitting here—going grocery shopping, cooking dinner, wondering whether to close my business, wondering what I would do with my life if I did. If I didn't have my business, then what was I doing?

Somehow, when I lost my sole source of income, I fell into a rut that I'm sure so many people fell into during the pandemic, and one that I thought I was immune to: not only is our healthcare tied to our jobs, but our self-worth is as well. In 2021 I took so many steps backward. I took my wonderful husband and incredible group of friends for granted. I forgot how much joy they bring into my life. I fell into traps of doubt and anxiety and second-guessing myself. I was lost and despondent; I stopped caring about cooking dinner or getting dressed most days or anything else. I started giving a fuck about all the things I was never supposed to and forgot about all the things that mattered most. Day after day I would heave heavy sighs, and when my husband would ask what's wrong, I would utter the same refrain: "I don't know what the fuck I'm doing with my life."

And then in January, I started writing this book again. And I remembered all those things I had somehow let myself forget: That my worth isn't tied to any external success, and it never will be. That I don't really give a fuck about that when it comes down to it. That I don't have to be successful or famous or anything else to be happy. That we have lived on so much less than we have now, that we survived when I was making $1,000 a month, that I survived living on even less than that—and that we can always do it again. I don't know what I'll do when I finish writing this book. I don't have any plans or answers. But what I do have is a reminder that I am surrounded by people who I love who return that love to me. If I have to work in a bar again or clean toilets again or whatever else, then that's what I'll do. Because all this time I was letting myself forget that I already had everything I ever needed.

If we're doing it right, we're always growing. And some times are easy and some times are hard. Sometimes you eat the bear, and sometimes, well, he eats you. But when you find yourself falling back into those same traps, take a step back. Remember how little most of these things matter in the grand scheme of things. Try to remember that no one is perfect, that nothing is black and white in this world, and that all any of us can do is our best. Find the gratitude for the things you do have and remember life will always be okay as long as you're okay with whatever life is. So few of our problems today will matter tomorrow, even fewer will matter in six months, and a year from now, we won't even remember what most of them were. Love and be loved. Gratitude and validation. Put out into the world what you want to get back. And if you really can't remember what matters on this earth, then you can always fall back on Carl Sagan.

As the Voyager spaceship was hurtling out into the unexplored nether regions of outer space, farther than any manmade object had ever flown, Carl Sagan suggested to NASA that they turn it around back towards Earth and snap a photo. The photo that was taken from six billion kilometers away (3.7 billion miles) shows a vast, black nothingness with a single, tiny pinprick of pale blue light. The pinprick, that single pixel, is our planet. Here is an excerpt from Sagan's 1994 book, *Pale Blue Dot*:

> From this distant vantage point, the Earth might not seem of any particular interest. But for us, it's different. Consider again that dot. That's here. That's home. That's us. On it everyone you love, everyone you know, everyone you ever heard of, every human being who ever was, lived out their lives. The aggregate of our joy and suffering, thousands of confident religions, ideologies, and economic doctrines, every hunter and forager, every hero and coward, every creator and destroyer of civilization, every king and peasant, every young couple in love, every mother and father, hopeful child, inventor and explorer, every teacher of morals, every corrupt politician, every "superstar," every "supreme leader," every saint and sinner in the history of our species lived there—on a mote of dust suspended in a sunbeam.
>
> The Earth is a very small stage in a vast cosmic arena. Think of the rivers of blood spilled by all those generals and emperors so that, in glory and triumph, they could become the momentary masters of a fraction of a dot. Think of the endless cruelties visited by the inhabitants of one corner of this pixel on the scarcely distinguishable inhabitants of some

other corner, how frequent their misunderstandings, how eager they are to kill one another, how fervent their hatreds.

Our posturings, our imagined self-importance, the delusion that we have some privileged position in the Universe, are challenged by this point of pale light. Our planet is a lonely speck in the great enveloping cosmic dark. In our obscurity, in all this vastness, there is no hint that help will come from elsewhere to save us from ourselves.

The Earth is the only world known so far to harbor life. There is nowhere else, at least in the near future, to which our species could migrate. Visit, yes. Settle, not yet. Like it or not, for the moment the Earth is where we make our stand.

It has been said that astronomy is a humbling and character-building experience. There is perhaps no better demonstration of the folly of human conceits than this distant image of our tiny world. To me, it underscores our responsibility to deal more kindly with one another, and to preserve and cherish the pale blue dot, the only home we've ever known.

Whenever you get wrapped up in your own bullshit, read this passage again. When I read it, I remember that nothing we do will ever truly matter in the universe. There are humans who will go down in history as great, brilliant humans; geniuses like Einstein and da Vinci and maybe even the man or woman who one day cures cancer or solves global warming and saves the only planet we have. But at the end of it all, no matter what you achieve during your time on this planet, the only thing that will really have mattered is love. The only truly indelible mark you leave is in the hearts and memories of the people who loved you. The rest of everything will one day be dust.

When I ponder the meaning of life, when I think about the inevitable extinction of the human race, I always come to this same simple conclusion. And I'm not just talking about the comforting solidity of a married love or the fevered highs of new infatuation—I mean all love. Love in all the ways the Greeks had words for. Love between your siblings and love between your friends. Love for every human you encounter. Approaching the world with love and positivity and making it that much better to be in.

We are tiny, meaningless specs in the great span of existence and the universe, and the only things that matter are the relationships that you foster and how much you make out of the insignificant time we have. Some people take that information and become nihilists or existentialists, believing that nothing matters. But the other way is to let it crystallize the one thing that does: here and now. There is a philosophical term called optimistic nihilism—nothing actually matters in the universe, so you get to create that meaning yourself. Because there is no real answer to the question, "why are we here?" we get to be here for whatever the fuck we want to be. To love, to be happy, to have a good fucking time. We have to find our own meaning in this world, and maybe, at the end of the day, that is the fucking point.

It's possible that this book has felt to you like two different books, and it does to me too. I spent the first half telling you that you could just fuck off and move to Paris, and the second half telling you that you wouldn't be happy if you did. But hopefully you understand that the core of the truth is that you will be happy in anything that you do so long as you are honest with yourself and others, so long as human relationships are what you prize above all else. So long as you live your life open to love of all kinds. And sure, move to Paris while you're at it.

The end of the story is to find your meaning. If you are being honest with yourself and others, if you are finding what makes you truly happy in life—even if that's sitting on your ass playing video games—you will find happiness in Paris or Des Moines or in a van down by the river. If you are cultivating positive human relationships, congratulations, that's it. You don't have to have kids. You don't have to climb the corporate ladder.

You don't have to make a bunch of money or travel the world or do anything you don't want to do. All you really have to do is love and be loved. And the only way to do that is to be your weird, unique, one-of-a-kind, authentic self.

one last thing

When I started writing this book in 2017, I wasn't quite sure what it was going to be. Honestly, after reading so many mediocre self-help books that pretty much all said the same things, I felt like I could jam one out pretty quickly. But as I wrote, I found more and more of myself in the words I was writing. I realized that no book about finding happiness can exist without real vulnerability—without practicing what you're preaching. So, instead of jamming out the fastest book I could, I poured a lot more of myself into this than I expected.

I know it's not perfect. If you've made it this far, thank you for tolerating my penchant for verbosity and addiction to both emdashes and serial lists. But either way, I wrote a motherfucking book. And, as ever, there are a few more people to thank.

Thank you to my friend and colleague, Walter—the first person to read it when it was definitely still a "steaming pile of shit" who helped me to see all the ways I could make it better. Thanks to Ellen and Heather and Fernanda who helped me make it even better when I was too stubbornly frugal to pay a professional editor to do it.

Thank you to all the friends who've loved me for being me—who've allowed me to express myself and be myself without judgment (unless it was warranted), who've shown me what real, wondrous, virtuous relationships look like, and who've shown me that there will always be someone to love you if you come at the world with honesty, authenticity, and kindness.

And thank you to my astounding husband, Hudson, who encouraged me to put myself out into the world and share my secrets, even though I know it makes him terribly uncomfortable. I don't know who or what I'd be without you; I just know you make my life better every single day.

www.ingramcontent.com/pod-product-compliance
Lightning Source LLC
Chambersburg PA
CBHW030331010526
44119CB00036B/458/J